W9-BAY-327
BOYD COUNTY
AUG 2 1 2015
PUBLIC LIBRARY

THE CALL

THE LIFE AND MESSAGE OF THE APOSTLE PAUL

THE CALL

THE LIFE AND MESSAGE OF THE APOSTLE PAUL

The Call
978-1-630-88262-4
978-1-630-88263-1 *eBook*

The Call:
Large Print Edition
978-1-630-88264-8

The Call: DVD
978-1-630-88267-9

The Call: Leader Guide
978-1-630-88265-5
978-1-630-88266-2 *eBook*

The Call: Youth Study
978-1-630-88268-6
978-1-630-88269-3 *eBook*

The Call: Children's
Leader Guide
978-1-630-88270-9

For more information,
visit www.AdamHamilton.org

Also by Adam Hamilton

24 Hours That Changed the World

Christianity and World Religions

Christianity's Family Tree

Confronting the Controversies

Enough

Final Words from the Cross

Forgiveness

Leading Beyond the Walls

Love to Stay

Making Sense of the Bible

Not a Silent Night

Revival

Seeing Gray in a World of Black and White

Selling Swimsuits in the Arctic

The Journey

The Way

Unleashing the Word

When Christians Get It Wrong

Why?

Adam Hamilton

The Call

The Life and Message of the Apostle Paul

Abingdon Press
Nashville

THE CALL:
THE LIFE AND MESSAGE OF THE APOSTLE PAUL

Copyright © 2015 by Abingdon Press
All rights reserved.

No part of this work may be reproduced or transmitted in any form or by any means, electronic or mechanical, including photocopying and recording, or by any information storage or retrieval system, except as may be expressly permitted by the 1976 Copyright Act or in writing from the publisher. Requests for permission can be addressed to Permissions, The United Methodist Publishing House, P.O. Box 280988, Nashville, TN 37228-0988; 2222 Rosa L. Parks Boulevard, Nashville, TN 37228-1306; or e-mailed to permissions@umpublishing.org.

This book is printed on elemental, chlorine-free paper.

Library of Congress Cataloging-in-Publication Data applied for.

ISBN 978-1-630-88262-4

All Scripture quotations, unless otherwise indicated, are taken from New Revised Standard Version of the Bible, copyright 1989, Division of Christian Education of the National Council of the Churches of Christ in the United States of America. Used by permission. All rights reserved.

Scripture quotations noted CEB are from the Common English Bible. Copyright © 2011 by the Common English Bible. All rights reserved. Used by permission. www.CommonEnglishBible.com.

Scripture quotations marked (NIV) are taken from the Holy Bible, New International Version®, NIV®. Copyright © 1973, 1978, 1984, 2011 by Biblica, Inc.™ Used by permission of Zondervan. All rights reserved worldwide. www.zondervan.com. The "NIV" and "New International Version" are trademarks registered in the United States Patent and Trademark Office by Biblica, Inc.™

Scripture quotations from THE MESSAGE. Copyright © by Eugene H. Peterson 1993, 1994, 1995, 1996, 2000, 2001, 2002. Used by permission of NavPress Publishing Group.

Scripture quotations from The Authorized (King James) Version. Rights in the Authorized Version in the United Kingdom are vested in the Crown. Reproduced by permission of the Crown's patentee, Cambridge University Press.

15 16 17 18 19 20 21 22 23—10 9 8 7 6 5 4 3 2 1
MANUFACTURED IN THE UNITED STATES OF AMERICA

In memory of Pastor Phil Hollis,
who helped me to hear God's call to
follow Jesus and then encouraged me
to answer God's call to be a pastor.
I am forever indebted to him.

CONTENTS

INTRODUCTION

It could reasonably be argued that no other human, apart from Jesus himself, has had a greater impact on the world than Paul of Tarsus. His theological reflections on the meaning of Jesus' life, death, and resurrection have had a profound impact upon every branch of the Christian faith. His missionary journeys took the gospel across the Roman world. He mentored many second-generation Christian leaders. Thirteen of the New Testament's twenty-seven books are attributed to him, and one-half of the Acts of the Apostles is devoted to telling his story. Today, one-third of the world's population look to his writings for inspiration, spiritual direction, and ethical guidance, more than follow the teachings of Muhammad, the Buddha, and Confucius combined.

Yet Paul is not without his critics. Jews typically see Paul as a misguided and even apostate first-century Jew who misrepresented Judaism and whose writings contributed to anti-Semitism over the centuries.* Jews view him as the founder of

* I appreciate Professor Mark Nanos's perspective on Paul that both Jews and Christians have likely misunderstood Paul at points. Nanos is a Jewish Pauline scholar. See his chapter, "A Jewish View," in *Four Views on the Apostle Paul*, ed. Michael F. Bird (Grand Rapids: Zondervan, 2012).

Christianity, transforming the life and teachings of Jesus, a rabbi and reformer within Judaism, into a divine redeemer and object of worship. Muslims often see Paul as one who corrupted the teachings of Jesus, trying to turn a man whom they regard as a prophet into the divine Son of God. Many Christians believe that Paul's teaching regarding women—that they were to be submissive to their husbands (Colossians 3:18), that they were not to teach in the church (1 Corinthians 14:34), that they were to "learn in quietness and submission" (1 Timothy 2:11)—contributed to centuries of women's subordination. In passages such as Romans 1:26-28, gay and lesbian people see words that led countless men and women to be treated as shameful for loving persons of the same gender. In centuries past, Paul's words were regularly quoted in support of slavery and God's approval of it.

It is clear in reading the New Testament that even in the first-century church, Paul had his critics. We get hints of Paul's conflicts with Peter and James. Some Jewish followers of Jesus, particularly those called "Judaizers" or the "circumcision party," vehemently opposed Paul and rejected his teaching that circumcision and obedience to the Law were no longer required of Christ's followers. And of course, for reasons stated above that persist in our time, mainstream Jewish leaders found his teaching offensive and blasphemous.

Christians today will reject some claims of Paul's critics but may recognize truth in others. For example, Christians recognize that Paul offers an interpretation of Jesus' life, death, and resurrection that became normative within Christianity, but we reject the claim that his theologizing about Jesus was a corruption of Jesus' life and teachings. We recognize that Paul's teachings about slaves being obedient to their masters or women being silent in the church have sometimes been used to destructive ends in Christian circles. New Testament scholars of the so-called "new perspectives on Paul" acknowledge that typical interpretations of Paul's writings concerning the Law and first-century Judaism may not accurately reflect Paul's true views on those subjects.

For me, many of these critiques are mitigated by recognizing that Paul was a man of his times. Paul was shaped by his childhood, his education and experiences, his profound conversion, and his years spent reflecting upon the meaning and implications of Jesus' life, death, and resurrection. The context for his ministry was the Greco-Roman world of the first century. He was educated both in the currents of Greek philosophy and in a specific school of thought that was part of first-century Judaism. His understanding of the gospel was molded by his own faith crises and spiritual experiences. In this, Paul is little different from any of us.

When we read Paul's letters, we see his humanity shining through. He is not simply a mouthpiece of the Holy Spirit; he is a man who has strong convictions, is aware of his critics, and regularly defends himself against them. At times he gets angry and defensive. He has physical ailments and has faced his share of adversity. He is a devout Jew whose thinking is completely immersed in the Greek translation of the Hebrew Scriptures. He is a Roman citizen aware of the events and ethos of the empire. He is familiar with the Greek philosophers and poets. Though a brilliant and skilled orator and philosopher, his theological arguments are sometimes confusing and difficult to grasp. At times he is a pastor seeking to encourage his converts and address their needs; at other times he is a politician trying to navigate among religious parties and between two worlds—the Greco-Roman world and the world of first-century Judaism. Through it all, he seeks to be an apostle and disciple of Jesus Christ, proclaiming the good news as he understands it.

I have a deep appreciation for Paul. His story inspires me. His writings have shaped my life more than any but the Gospels. Though I'm aware of his shortcomings and at times disagree with him, I believe his life, when viewed as a whole, reveals a heroic figure who sought to exemplify what it means to faithfully follow Jesus Christ. I believe God still speaks through his words, nearly two thousand years after they were written, in order to help us know Christ and live as his followers.

My hope in writing this book is to share Paul's story, hear his message, and reflect on the meaning of his life and message for our own lives and our world today. In preparing to write, I reread Paul's story in Acts several times. I reread Paul's letters in the New Testament. I read a host of books, both scholarly and popular, all listed in the bibliography. I journeyed with my wife and a film crew, retracing Paul's footsteps in Turkey, Greece, and Italy, traveling by plane, car, and boat some fourteen thousand miles, visiting many of the archaeological sites where Paul preached and taught.

This book will follow Paul's life chronologically. Bear in mind that there is some disagreement about when Paul was born, when he was converted, and when his travels took place. Some details of Paul's story in Acts are difficult to reconcile chronologically with what we find in Paul's letters. Precise dates in his life, therefore, are subject to debate.

To bring you along on my travels, in each chapter I'll include photos of places associated with the events described. I visited most of those places, though several were deemed too dangerous to visit at the time we were traveling, due to armed conflicts in the areas. For the places I was unable to visit, photographs were obtained from other sources. If you truly want to travel beside me, a DVD is available for individual or group use in which I take readers to many of the archaeological sites where Paul preached and founded churches.

There are many excellent scholarly books on Paul and many tremendous commentaries on the Acts of the Apostles. At the back of this book, I've listed a number of them that I've read and drawn upon in preparation for this study. My aim in this book, however, is not to write another commentary but rather to draw upon and distill many of the scholars' insights. More than that,

I hope what sets this book apart is the way I've sought to connect Paul's life and message to the reader's life and faith. Throughout the book I invite the reader to ask, "How does this part of Paul's story speak to my life today?" In the end, my aim is not simply to teach about Paul, but to help modern-day Christians deepen their own faith and answer God's call upon their lives by studying Paul's life, story, and call.

1
Called to Follow Christ

Paul's Background, Conversion, and Early Ministry

[And Paul said,] "I am a Jew, born in Tarsus in Cilicia... a citizen of an important city... circumcised on the eighth day, a member of the people of Israel, of the tribe of Benjamin, a Hebrew born of Hebrews... brought up in [Jerusalem] at the feet of Gamaliel, educated strictly according to our ancestral law being zealous for God... I advanced in Judaism beyond many among my people of the same age... I persecuted this Way up to the point of death by binding both men and women and putting them in prison."

—Acts 22:3a, 21:39b, Philippians 3:5, Acts 22:3b, Galatians 1:14a, Acts 22:4

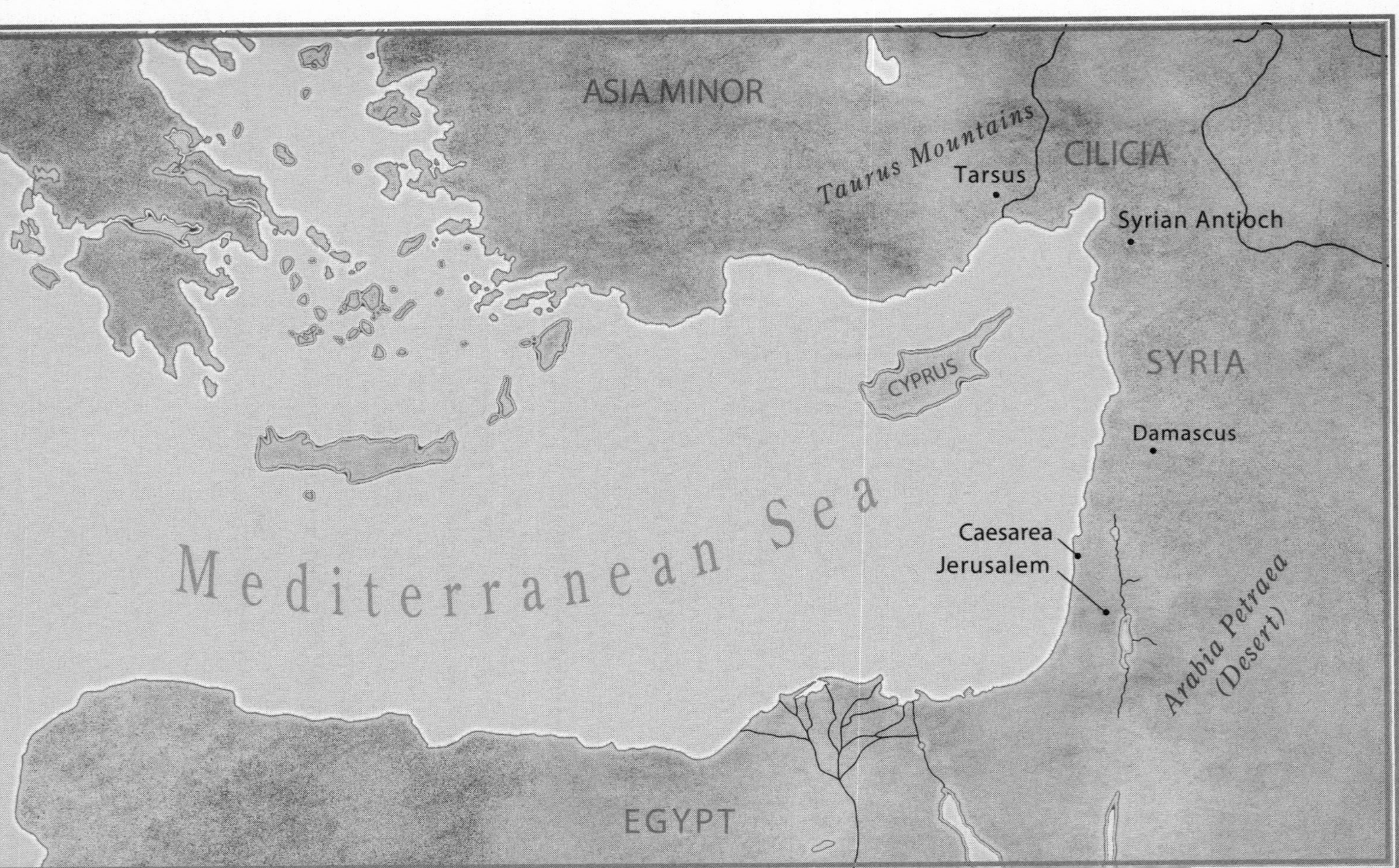

ASIA MINOR
Taurus Mountains
Tarsus
CILICIA
Syrian Antioch
SYRIA
CYPRUS
Damascus
Mediterranean Sea
Caesarea
Jerusalem
Arabia Petraea
(Desert)
EGYPT

A.D. 67 Paul's Death

5 B.C. - A.D. 10 Paul is Born (est.)

65

60

55

50

45

40

A.D. 38-48 Paul in Tarsus and region (est.)

A.D. 38 Paul meets Peter and James in Jerusalem

A.D. 35-38 Paul in Arabia, then Damascus

35

A.D. 35 Paul is converted on road to Damascus (est.)

A.D. 32 Paul arrests Jesus followers in Palestine (est.)

30

25

20

A.D. 16-22 Paul begins study in Jerusalem (est.)

15

5 B.C.-A.D.10 Paul is born (est.)

HIS PARENTS NAMED HIM SAUL, after the first king of Israel who, like their child, was of the tribe of Benjamin. His father and mother were part of the Jewish diaspora, living in Tarsus, a major city in the eastern part of the Roman Empire, with what may have been as many as two hundred thousand residents.*

Tarsus was located ten miles from the Mediterranean Sea on the plateau between the Taurus Mountains and the sea. You could get there by ship traveling up the Cydnus River to a harbor leading into the city. It was a magnificent city, cooled by a sea breeze and nestled at the base of the mountains.

In earlier times, Tarsus had been the capital of the region called Cilicia; by Paul's time, though no longer the capital, Tarsus was still a very important city. Caesar Augustus had granted it special status as a "free city," a way of ensuring the loyalty of its citizens. This was particularly important because Tarsus was located on a key east–west trade route bringing goods from the east to the interior of Asia Minor (modern-day Turkey). This ancient highway passed through the famous Cilician Gates, a mountain pass to the north of Tarsus. As citizens of a free city, the people of Tarsus were permitted to govern themselves, were allowed to mint their own coins, and were free from most Roman taxes.[1] (As you can imagine, avoiding Roman taxes was a tremendous draw, and people were eager to move there.)†

There's little left for us to see of Tarsus from Paul's time. Much of the modern city was built atop previous cities that were built atop even earlier cities; hence, the ruins of Paul's Tarsus are mostly buried beneath the present city. Two exceptions include

* The estimated population for cities in the Roman Empire during the first century A.D. is difficult to ascertain with certainty. Different sources will offer differing numbers. The ancient ruins of Tarsus are largely buried beneath the modern city, making it even more difficult to estimate. Throughout the book I will use numbers that are derived from multiple sources and will generally go with more conservative estimates. Estimates I've seen for the population of Tarsus in the first century range from one hundred thousand to five hundred thousand people.

† Dio Chrysostom, a younger contemporary of Paul, noted the cost of Tarsian citizenship was five hundred drachma, a drachma being a common laborer's daily wage.

The Taurus Mountains run along much of the southern coast of Turkey. Paul grew up seeing these mountains and passed through them at some point on each of his missionary journeys.

a section of Roman road within the city and an old well referred to as St. Paul's Well, which is adjacent to excavated ruins said to be Paul's childhood home. The likelihood of these ruins being Paul's home seems remote to me, but these landmarks give visitors a place to anchor Paul's story.

We learn in the Book of Acts that Paul was born a Roman citizen (22:26), and yet it is estimated that only 10 percent of the empire's population at the time had been granted citizenship, perhaps significantly less in the eastern part of the empire. This leads us to believe that Paul's parents likely were wealthy or important landowners or business owners in Tarsus who themselves had been granted citizenship. It's also likely they were tentmakers or owned a tentmaking business, given that Paul himself was trained as a tentmaker.

Tarsus was an important intellectual center in the Roman Empire. Strabo, a Greek philosopher and geographer who died in A.D. 24, described Tarsus and its citizens this way:

> The inhabitants of this city apply to the study of philosophy and to the whole encyclical compass of learning with so much ardour, that they surpass Athens, Alexandria, and every other place which can be named where there are schools and lectures of philosophers.[2]

The Cilician Gates, a famous mountain pass near Tarsus, was a major trade route and has been enlarged in modern times. Paul would have passed through these "gates" on his second and third missionary journeys.

It was a place of culture and learning. It is likely that young Saul, whose Roman name was Paul, received instruction at the Greco-Roman primary and grammar schools of Tarsus up to the age of thirteen before being sent to study in Jerusalem. In these schools, Paul would have learned the art of writing and the use of language; he would have studied the Greek poets and the basics of Greek rhetoric and logic.[3] These studies would have played a pivotal role in preparing him at an early age for his later work as an apostle, Christianity's first theologian, and the man who would be credited with writing thirteen of the New Testament's twenty-seven books.

Though the practice of having a Bar Mitzvah at age thirteen began later than Paul's time, it may give some indication of when Jewish young men being prepared for rabbinical studies might have gone to Jerusalem to study. Similarly, the story of Jesus in the temple when he was twelve might point to an age at which boys in Paul's time were thought to become men and hence ready to learn from the great teachers in Judaism. It seems at least possible, then, that Paul was sent to Jerusalem by his parents sometime around his twelfth or thirteenth birthday, where he may have studied the Law, both written and oral, under Gamaliel I, one of the leading first-century rabbis, up to the age of twenty. For a first-century Jew, this may have been akin to our practice of going away to college.

Mention of Paul's age raises the question of when he was born, and to that we have no clear answer.* It is often said he was born sometime between 5 B.C. and A.D. 10. I lean more toward A.D. 10, which would mean that Paul finished his schooling under Gamaliel around A.D. 30, close to the year Jesus was crucified.† This fits nicely with the idea that young Paul was anxious to make a name for himself by persecuting the fledgling Christian movement.

How God Uses the Puzzle Pieces of Our Lives

You may wonder why these details of Paul's early life are important. The reason is that Paul and the things he would later think, write, say, and do were in part the result of his early life experiences. Think of Moses, who grew up in Pharaoh's household and thus was the ideal candidate for God to use in liberating the Israelite slaves from Egypt. In a similar way, Paul's childhood in a predominantly Gentile city known for its culture and outstanding Greco-Roman education, his tentmaking in his father's shop as a boy, his grasp of the Greek language, his Roman citizenship, his education by one of the leading rabbis of his day—all these experiences were critical to the work Paul one day would be called to as Christianity's leading apostle to the Greco-Roman world.

---

* There is great variance in opinion about when Paul was born and how old he was when we first meet him in Acts. Some have suggested he was as old as thirty-five or forty. But recognizing milestones in Jewish education and when Jewish boys were considered to become men, I believe he completed his studies around the age of twenty and persecuted the followers of Jesus shortly after that. In the end, any date given by a scholar will be conjecture.

† We don't know for certain when Jesus was born. It was probably 3 to 5 B.C. The dates of Jesus' birth being several years "before Christ" points to an error in our calendaring system.

Pause here for a moment and consider your own background—your family of origin, the experiences you had growing up, your education, and religious training. In what ways might God call you to use these things for his purposes?

I was baptized Roman Catholic as an infant, but we did not attend church much when I was small. My father was Catholic, and my mother was a member of the Church of Christ. When they married it was clear my father was not likely to join the Church of Christ, nor my mother the Roman Catholic Church. When I was in third grade, my parents struggled to find a church somewhere between those two, and they settled on the United Methodist Church. My parents eventually divorced, and we dropped out of church. My mom remarried a good man who had serious alcohol problems, so there was constant chaos at our house. My stepdad relocated our family from our childhood home to a southern suburb of Kansas City. It was there that I encountered Christ at a small Pentecostal church, met my future wife, and felt called to be a pastor. Marrying right out of high school, I went off to college at Oral Roberts University, where I received a great education in a charismatic, evangelical tradition. It was while in school at ORU that I felt called to rejoin The United Methodist Church and specifically to take part in revitalizing a church that had been in decline for twenty years by that time. Partly because of that experience, I attended seminary at Southern Methodist University, where I received excellent and somewhat liberal theological training.

Each part of what I've described above is a piece of the puzzle that shaped the person, pastor, and author I am today. I carry a Roman Catholic appreciation for tradition, a Pentecostal and charismatic belief in the power of the Holy Spirit, a compassion based on growing up with an alcoholic stepdad and an often chaotic home life, a willingness to see truth on both the left and the right shaped by my education at an evangelical undergraduate school and a liberal seminary. It is as if God looked at the various pieces of my life and said, "I can use each of those parts of your past, your life experience, and your faith if you'll let me."

In my experience, the most difficult or painful parts of my past are often the very things that have been the most important elements in whatever success I've had in ministry and in life to the present. In so many ways our lives are like puzzles, and God has a unique way of bringing those various pieces of the puzzle together to create something beautiful and useful in us. What are the puzzle pieces—the life experiences you've had—that God might use to accomplish his redemptive work in the world? God's call on our lives is often surprising and usually is based on God's ability to see how our various elements in the past might fit together to accomplish God's purposes in the present.

Saul the Persecutor

The first time we read about Paul's life in the Acts of the Apostles is in Chapter 7. Jesus had been crucified and resurrected and had ascended to heaven just a couple of years earlier. The fledgling movement of Christ's followers had exploded in Jerusalem. There now were thousands of people who believed that Jesus was in fact the long-awaited Messiah. These Jewish disciples of Jesus called themselves "followers of the Way," and among them, surprisingly, were some of the rabbis from the party of the Pharisees. In Acts 6 one of the leaders of the Way, a man named Stephen, was arrested and placed on trial. When he gave his testimony, the Jewish leaders in Jerusalem convicted him of blasphemy and condemned him to death. In Acts 7 we first hear Paul mentioned in Scripture, though by his Hebrew name:

> Then they dragged [Stephen] out of the city and began to stone him; and the witnesses laid their coats at the feet of a young man named Saul.... And Saul approved of their killing him. (Acts 7:58-60; 8:1)

It appears that Paul may have been about twenty years old at the time, which would mean he was quite young to be giving approval for the killing of Stephen.

Death by stoning required that the witness who testified against the convicted individual drop the first stones upon him. The fact that they laid their coats at Paul's feet likely indicates that Paul was given authority to act on behalf of the Jewish leaders to oversee the execution. The Mishnah, or first written version of what was called the Oral Torah, tells us what this process looked like. The victim would be thrown down on his back and held there. Standing over him, about ten feet above the ground on a platform, the first witness took a large stone and dropped it on the victim's chest. If the victim did not die after the first stone, a second was dropped by the second witness. If after the first two witnesses the victim did not die, those around would take rocks and strike him until he died.[4]

We read in Acts that after Stephen's death,

> That day a severe persecution began against the church in Jerusalem, and all except the apostles were scattered throughout the countryside of Judea and Samaria.... Saul was ravaging the church by entering house after house; dragging off both men and women, he committed them to prison.... Saul, still breathing threats and murder against the disciples of the Lord, went to the high priest and asked him for letters to the synagogues at Damascus, so that if he found any who belonged to the Way, men or women, he might bring them bound to Jerusalem. (Acts 8:1, 3; 9:1-2)

What was it that motivated Paul to volunteer for the job of approving Stephen's execution and then going from house to house to arrest followers of the Way? I think it may have been the same thing that caused him years later to write, "I advanced in Judaism beyond many among my people of the same age, for I was far more zealous for the traditions of my ancestors" (Galatians 1:14). Early in his career Paul was eager to impress the Jewish ruling council in Jerusalem and to make a name for himself. In other words, it was Paul's personal ambition, combined with his unwavering religious convictions, that I believe led him to the work of persecuting the fledgling Christian movement.

Thinking about ambition, let's consider once more how Paul's story might connect with your story or with the stories of people you may know. Many of us struggle with ambition. I have struggled with it my whole life. I remember praying years ago, "Lord, please take away my ambition." And I felt him saying to me, "I'm not going to take it away; I'm going to use it, but your ambition must be for me and not for you."

Some people are blinded by ambition and are willing at times to do horrible things in order to get ahead. Paul was convinced that followers of the Way, regardless of how devout or gentle or loving, had to be stopped. It wasn't God that drove him to arrest those followers and approve their deaths. Blind ambition and unwavering religious conviction can be a dangerous combination.

It's important for us to submit our ambition to God, directing it to his glory and not our own, and for the most part that's what Paul seems to have done for the rest of his life. We can avoid acts that are contrary to our faith, as Paul learned to do, by holding our religious convictions with humility and never forgetting the commands of loving God and neighbor. To help me with that task, I memorized Scripture—like Psalm 115:1, which I often repeat as a "breath prayer," (the kind of prayer you can say in one breath): "Not to us, O LORD, not to us, but to your name give glory." I committed to memory Jesus' question in Matthew 16:26, "What good will it be for someone to gain the whole world, yet forfeit their soul?" (NIV).

When we fail to surrender our ambition to God's purposes, when we live to seek our glory and are willing to do whatever it takes to get ahead, we are bound to fall. But if we succeed in surrendering our ambition to God's purposes, we will help others find their way on the path of life. That's exactly what Paul was about to do.

It Is Hard to Kick Against the Goads

Paul, with letters in hand from the high priest authorizing the arrest of followers of the Way, began his way to Damascus. While on the road, he was stopped in his tracks, and his life was changed forever. Here is how he described the experience:

> I was traveling to Damascus with the authority and commission of the chief priests, when at midday along the road…I saw a light from heaven, brighter than the sun, shining around me and my companions. When we had all fallen to the ground, I heard a voice saying to me in the Hebrew language, "Saul, Saul, why are you persecuting me? It hurts you to kick against the goads." I asked, "Who are you, Lord?" The Lord answered, "I am Jesus whom you are persecuting."
>
> (Acts 26:12-15)

Some have suggested the light from heaven was a bolt of lightning that struck near Paul and his colleagues. Whatever happened, it was terrifying, and Paul was blinded by it. In the midst of the light, Paul heard Jesus speaking to him. I love what Jesus said: "Saul, Saul…it hurts you to kick against the goads."

What on earth is a goad? A goad is a stick with a pointed end, used to prod oxen and cattle to move in the direction their owner wants them to go. Jesus was saying, in effect, that he had been prodding or "goading" Paul in the right direction for some time, that Paul had not paid attention, and that his failure to pay attention was hurting Paul and others. ("It hurts you to kick against the goads.")

What an interesting idea: God is prodding us on a regular basis, seeking to lead us, guide us, and move us to do his will and to live as his people. God's prod is gentle yet persistent. And yet, unlike the old farmer who goads his oxen so hard they can't help but obey, God allows us to resist his goading.

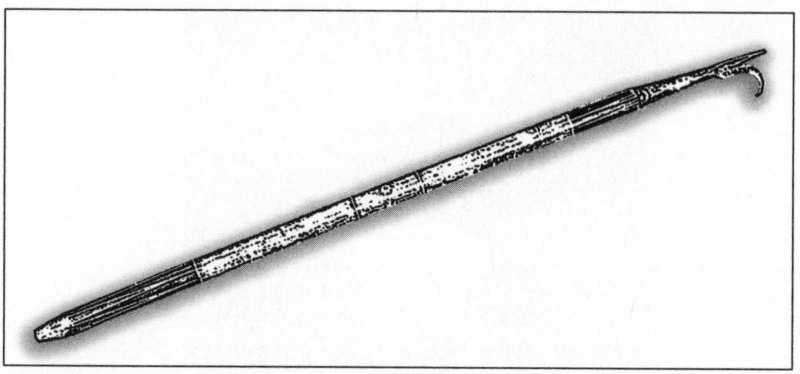

A goad is a stick with a sharp point at the end, and sometimes a hook, used to prod animals.

Pastor Dave Wilkinson wrote about this goading work of God. He and his wife were on a plane, sitting next to a young man who asked, "So, what do you do?" Wilkinson told him, "I'm a minister." The young man nearly jumped out of his seat and then said, "Every time I sit next to someone, he turns out to be a Christian. I can't escape. I know that God is after me." Wilkinson told him that he was probably right and "the only smart thing to do in such a situation is to surrender."[5]

I wonder if you've felt God's nudges, pokes, and proddings. Are you being goaded by God? Are you paying attention? Or, like Dave Wilkinson and his wife, are you being called by God to be a gentle nudge, a reminder to someone else, that God is chasing after him?

The Importance of Ananias

Paul, temporarily blinded, was led by his fellow travelers to Damascus. This lion of a man, who had breathed murderous threats against the church of Jesus, now was led, terrified, to a home on Straight Street. If you visit Damascus today, you can go to the old city and see Straight Street, marked at one end by a triumphal Roman arch.

Roman arch at Straight Street

Paul sat there for three days, unable to see, his physical blindness a way of helping him see his previous spiritual blindness. He was unwilling to eat or drink. God was working on him in the silence as he came face to face with a disturbing fact: his desire to serve God had been distorted by his own ambition, which had led him to persecute God's people.

Meanwhile, God was prodding someone else, a man named Ananias, who was a follower of Christ and someone whom Paul likely had come to arrest. Christ spoke to Ananias in a vision. We aren't told the precise nature of this prod—perhaps it was a dream, an idea, a strong urging from within, a still small voice.

The Lord said to him, "Get up and go to the street called Straight, and at the house of Judas look for a man of Tarsus named Saul."...But Ananias answered, "Lord, I have heard from many about this man, how much evil he has done to your saints." (Acts 9:11, 13)

Christ told Ananias to find the house where Paul was staying, then to pray for Paul so that he might see again. Understandably, Ananias was afraid and objected, but the voice of Christ persisted, so finally Ananias went. Imagine the courage it must have taken for Ananias to confront Paul the inquisitor.

Ananias went and entered the house. He laid his hands on Saul and said, "Brother Saul, the Lord Jesus, who appeared to you on your way here, has sent me so that you may regain your sight and be filled with the Holy Spirit." And immediately something like scales fell from his eyes, and his sight was restored. Then he got up and was baptized. (Acts 9:17-18)

Today in Damascus, Paul's baptism is remembered in a small church said to be built on the site of Ananias's home. The house sits fifteen feet below ground level, where the street would have been located 1,900 years ago.

Notice that Paul's conversion was a result both of his experience of Christ and of Ananias sharing with him. This is how it often works. Most of us don't have a Damascus Road blinding-light conversion, but we do experience Christ in some way: we feel him speaking to us, we sense his love, we feel

Ananias's House Chapel in Damascus. Tradition says that this chapel was built atop the home of Ananias.

moved to say yes. But we also have our Ananiases who come alongside to offer us Christ.

We never again hear about Ananias in the Bible. He courageously stepped up, went to Paul, and shared Christ with him, and as a result the world was changed.

As for Paul, he learned that conversion happens to us when we stop pursuing our own blind ambition, when we recognize God's prodding in our lives, and when we finally surrender to God's will. That's where the real adventure begins. It certainly began there for Paul.

Beginning to Preach

It is impossible to overstate the impact that Paul's Damascus Road experience, along with his subsequent conversion and baptism, had on the young rabbi known as Saul. He was perhaps twenty-five years old at the time. He had had the finest of Greek and Jewish educations. He was on the fast track to becoming a real "somebody" in Judaism. Did he and his parents dare to dream that one day he might be the first Tarsian Jew to become part of the Sanhedrin, the Jewish ruling council?

In a moment, everything he had believed, all his ambitions and dreams, and all his life's work and preparation were upended by a flash of light and a voice. With the courageous help of Ananias, a disciple of Jesus in Damascus, Paul embraced the One whose voice he had heard. Paul began to eat, he was baptized, and his eyes were opened, literally and spiritually. And he began to preach. Here's what happened next:

> For several days he was with the disciples in Damascus, and immediately he began to proclaim Jesus in the synagogues, saying, "He is the Son of God." All who heard him were amazed and said, "Is not this the man who made havoc in Jerusalem among those who invoked this name? And has he not come here for the purpose of bringing them bound before the chief priests?" Saul became increasingly more powerful

> and confounded the Jews who lived in Damascus by proving that Jesus was the Messiah. (Acts 9:19b-22)

What a radical shift, from persecutor of the Way to its most powerful advocate! It was precisely this radical conversion that made Saul such a compelling witness. My own experience in speaking with atheists and agnostics is that it is impossible to reason and argue most people to faith. In the end, the most compelling case I can make for faith is my experiences of God's presence and how faith in Christ has made me a different person. I can point to hundreds of other people who once were addicts or self-centered narcissists or driven materialists or lying and cheating spouses whose lives have been changed in dramatic and positive ways by their trust in Christ.

Paul's education allowed him to offer a compelling and powerful case from Scripture for why Jesus was in fact the Christ, but it likely was his experience of Christ and his conversion that could not be argued away. He once was blind, but now he saw. He once persecuted the Way, but he had been seized by Christ on the road to Damascus, had been baptized, and now was willing to die for his faith. Early in his ministry, that willingness nearly was tested.

> After some time had passed, the Jews plotted to kill him, but their plot became known to Saul. They were watching the gates day and night so that they might kill him; but his disciples took him by night and let him down through an opening in the wall, lowering him in a basket. (Acts 9:23-25)

He who had persecuted the followers of the Way was now himself persecuted.

A Side Note About "the Jews"

I want to pause here for an important side note about terminology that was used by Luke, the author of Acts. Throughout the Book of Acts, Luke refers to those who opposed the gospel and sought to suppress Christianity as "the Jews." The phrase appears at least forty-four times in Acts, almost always negatively. John's Gospel uses the same term for those who opposed Jesus, with the phrase appearing at least sixty times in his Gospel. Unfortunately, use of the term would contribute to an anti-Semitism that reared its head throughout church history. "The Jews" became the killers of Christ and the persecutors of the church. Lost was the fact that Jesus was a Jew, the disciples were Jews, Paul was a Jew, and nearly all the thousands of Christ's followers at the time of Paul's conversion were Jews.

Had Luke and John known the impact their language would have and the anti-Semitism it would foster, I believe they would have chosen a different term. They were not referring to all Jews, nor even to most Jews, but to a small number of Jewish leaders who actively sought to suppress Jesus' message (in John) or the early church (in Acts). Some scholars believe that use of the phrase may have been a sign of strained relations between normative Judaism and the church during the time when Acts and John were written—Acts and John likely both being written in the 80s, when in some communities Jewish Christians were no longer welcome in the synagogue.

If you're not Jewish, use of this phrase may seem a small thing, but I believe it is important to note. Imagine if every act of anti-Semitism committed by someone claiming to be a Christian was attributed to "the Christians," or every hateful anti-gay sign was attributed to "the Christians." If we imagine this language ultimately leading to a broader persecution of all Christians, maybe we can begin to understand the negative impact this kind of generalizing language can have.[6]

Paul's Sojourn in Arabia and Back in Damascus

Paul reports in Galatians 1:17 that after escaping Damascus, "I went away at once into Arabia, and afterwards I returned to Damascus." Here Arabia refers to an area also known as Arabia Petraea—that is, the desert kingdom whose capital was Petra and whose territory included the Sinai Peninsula to the south, modern-day Jordan, and the desert regions in the east of modern-day Lebanon and Syria. In this region there were oasis cities, but much of the kingdom was in biblical terms the "wilderness."

The city of Petra in Jordan, whose buildings were carved out of the cliffs, may have been visited by Paul during his desert sojourn.

Moses and Elijah sojourned for a time in the wilderness, as did John the Baptist. Jesus spent forty days in prayer there. In much the same way, Paul fled Damascus for the wilderness. In Galatians he reports that he spent a total of three years in Arabia and back in Damascus, so we can't be sure how long he spent in the wilderness, nor what he was doing, but we might speculate. It may well be that the three-year period was spent reflecting upon the meaning of what had just happened to him.

My own belief is that Paul spent the three years beginning to work out his theology. The Benedictine monk and philosopher

St. Anselm (1033–1109) said the task of theology was "faith seeking understanding." I believe that is precisely what Paul was working out. He had had a profound, life-changing experience. He had encountered the risen Christ. But what were the implications of his encounter? How was he to make sense of his experience in the light of everything he knew about the Torah and the prophets? For three years (interestingly, the same period of time the disciples were said to have spent with Jesus—and the length of the typical Master of Divinity program in American theological seminaries), Paul spent time alone in prayer, studying the Scriptures, and seeking to work out the meaning of Jesus' life, death, and resurrection for humanity, with implications for both Jews and Gentiles.

The great theological themes of Paul's preaching and letters were not taught to him by someone else but, according to Paul himself, received by revelation from Christ. This revelation did not happen in just that one encounter on the Damascus Road; it took place over a period of time as Paul prayed, studied, and sought God.

> For I want you to know, brothers and sisters, that the gospel that was proclaimed by me is not of human origin; for I did not receive it from a human source, nor was I taught it, but I received it through a revelation of Jesus Christ.
>
> (Galatians 1:11-12)

Some have suggested that Paul spent the three years preaching and starting churches in Arabia, in what would have been his first foray as a missionary. This is possible, and perhaps it's likely that he did so at some point. But Luke doesn't mention it, and neither does Paul. Instead, the implication in these biblical texts is that Paul devoted time to study, prayer, and making sense of Jesus as the long-awaited Messiah, one who was crucified, dead, and buried, yet rose on the third day, conquering evil, hate, sin, and death. Paul had to rethink everything he had been taught about the Messiah, about the Law, about righteousness, and much more. I believe much of Paul's theology was worked out during this three-year "silent" period of his life, when he was in his late twenties.

The three-year silent period reminds me that we all must have times of silence and solitude for study, prayer, reflection, and listening for God's voice. For me this happens in reading Scripture and thoughtful books on faith. It happens in long walks when I seek to carry on conversations with Christ. It happens when I'm listening to the preaching of others and when I'm preparing my own sermons. It happens in times of personal retreat. It was part of the reason I traveled to Turkey, Greece, and Italy to retrace Paul's steps

All of us need silent times away to seek understanding, to have a flash of insight, or to hear the whisper of God's Spirit. Without those times, I find that my prayer life becomes anemic and I rarely listen for God to speak. I quickly hurry through my morning devotions because the clock is ticking and I've got work to do.

When was the last time you took time away from the busyness of your life for solitude, reading, prayer, and reflection? I find that such times refresh my soul and bring new visions and dreams that fill my heart. The times when God seems most distant to me, when I feel most spiritually empty, are when I haven't taken adequate time for spiritual retreat, reading, and prayer.

Paul and Peter: An Uncomfortable Relationship?

Paul reports in Galatians that after three years, "I did go up to Jerusalem to visit Cephas (Peter) and stayed with him fifteen days" (Galatians 1:18-19). In Acts 9, Luke seems to be describing this same time in Paul's life.

> When he had come to Jerusalem, he attempted to join the disciples; and they were all afraid of him, for they did not believe that he was a disciple. But Barnabas took him, brought him to the apostles, and described for them how on the road he had seen the Lord, who had spoken to him, and how in Damascus he had spoken boldly in the name of Jesus.
>
> (Acts 9:26-27)

Prior to his conversion, Paul had given approval for the stoning of Stephen and was "breathing threats and murder against the disciples of the Lord." It is no wonder that, even though they had received word three years earlier that Paul had come to faith, the disciples were suspicious and less than welcoming of Paul. It was Barnabas, of whom we'll speak more in a moment, who opened the door for Paul to meet with Peter, and not only to meet with him but also to stay in his home for fifteen days.

How I would love to have been a fly on the wall during Paul's fifteen days with Peter! Peter was an uneducated fisherman who knew Jesus personally and was one of his closest associates. Peter had three years' worth of firsthand stories about Jesus' life and teachings and his death and resurrection. Paul was highly educated both in the Scriptures and in Greek thought, and he had spent three years reflecting on the significance of Jesus in the light of that education. Yet he had never met the Jesus who walked on this earth in the flesh. Both Peter and Paul had important pieces of the gospel from which the other could benefit.

It is interesting to note that Paul, in his preaching and letters, devoted very little time to telling stories about Jesus' life. He offered very few direct quotes from Jesus' teachings (though he did make a few allusions to things Jesus said). It may be that Paul assumed these things were known by word-of-mouth to his hearers and readers (word-of-mouth because the earliest Gospels as we have them were likely not written until after the death of Paul). How grateful we should be that, in God's providence, we have both the Gospel accounts and the letters of Paul, each of which complements the other. The Gospel accounts describe events from the life of Jesus and the Lord's teachings, whereas Paul's focus is on the significance of Jesus' life and message, with a particular focus on the meaning of Jesus' death and resurrection.

It's easy to imagine that because of their differing perspectives, there was tension between these, Paul and Peter. My guess is that both were "alpha males." If Paul were, as I've suggested, ten to fifteen years Peter's junior, Paul might have felt a bit insecure around Peter. Paul's letter to the Galatians reveals this tension in two passages. In the first passage, Paul referred to the leaders of the Jerusalem church in this way: "Those who were supposed to be acknowledged leaders (what they actually were makes no difference to me; God shows no partiality)—those leaders contributed nothing to me" (2:6). In the second passage, Paul issued a public rebuke of Peter (Cephas) when Peter visited Syrian Antioch, saying "I opposed him to his face" (2:11). Whether or not Paul was in the right concerning Peter's error, the public rebuke seemed to lack the respect that should have been afforded to Jesus' lead apostle, and I think it may have been influenced by a feeling of jealousy or insecurity on Paul's part.

I am grateful that Paul included passages such as these in his letter to the Galatians. The passages demonstrate Paul's humanity—a man deeply devoted to God, courageously proclaiming the gospel, and yet imperfect like all of us, influenced by insecurities and occasionally acting in ways that do not reflect grace. I realize that some readers may feel uncomfortable when I suggest that Paul may have lacked tact or may have spoken out of insecurity. Who am I to judge Paul? Paul was an amazing man, a giant of a man—but he was still a man, and by his own words he seems at times to have lacked grace. Paul's flaws make me appreciate him even more, not simply as a mouthpiece for God but as a real man who was, like all of us, on the journey toward sanctification.

Whatever disagreements may have existed between Paul and Peter, the fact remains that on Paul's first visit to Jerusalem in three years, he spent fifteen days in Peter's home. Acts tells us that during Paul's visit,

> He went in and out among them in Jerusalem, speaking boldly in the name of the Lord. He spoke and argued with the Hellenists; but they were attempting to kill him. When the believers learned of it, they brought him down to Caesarea and sent him off to Tarsus. (Acts 9:28-30)

The In-Between Time

Barnabas and the other believers put Paul on a boat to Tarsus; he was moving back home in his late twenties. The son who was destined for greatness, who was educated in the finest schools in Tarsus and Jerusalem, likely moved back into his parent's house. How many young adults today can relate to this story? Paul's return must have caused confusion and disappointment for his parents, and possibly for Paul. We don't know how long he lived there. In Galatians 2:1, he notes that "after fourteen years I went up again to Jerusalem," but there is some confusion as to when the fourteen years started and whether or not it included Paul's first missionary journey. At the very least it appears that Paul lived in Tarsus for upwards of ten years after his conversion.

During that time, Paul likely used Tarsus as his home base, preaching and teaching at synagogues and fledgling churches in the regions of Cilicia and Syria, in what today is southeast Turkey. Note, however, that Paul had been told by the Lord at his conversion that he had an important mission to fulfill, and yet for at least ten years Paul lived in Tarsus, likely in his parents' home as he made tents in his father's business.

Paul's Well, Tarsus. Though Paul may never have drawn water from the well that bears his name, it is a physical reminder that Tarsus was Paul's hometown.

While living at home, Paul certainly must have continued to contemplate the meaning of the gospel. He undoubtedly grew in wisdom, which included both head and heart knowledge gained through lived experience. I've found that often the greatest wisdom-building experiences are those that come in the midst of disappointment, adversity, and waiting. Our faith often grows deeper, though we may not recognize it at the time. We don't know if Paul was experiencing a "dark night of the soul" during these ten years, but surely he wondered what had happened to the dramatic call he had heard from Ananias: "You will be [God's] witness to all the world of what you have seen and heard" (Acts 22:15).

It is interesting to note how often in Scripture there is a delay between the moment of God's call or an experience of God's presence or a vision that seems to come from God about the future and when these things actually come to pass. Consider Abraham, who was told in Genesis 12 that God would make him "a great nation," and in Genesis 22 that his descendants would be "as numerous as the stars of heaven." Abraham was seventy-five when he first heard God's call and promises. But it was nine chapters later, when Abraham was one hundred years old that Isaac was finally born. There were some challenging years in those nine chapters. The twenty-five years between the vision and fulfillment were the "in-between" time for Abraham and Sarah.

Consider Joseph, Abraham's great-grandson, who at the age of seventeen had visions of greatness he could not understand and did not handle well. It was only after being sold as a slave and later being cast into prison that Joseph finally became Pharaoh's right-hand man at the age of thirty, and it was another seven years before he was vindicated and the visions he had had at seventeen finally were fulfilled, at age thirty-seven. Those twenty years were the "in-between" time for Joseph.

Moses, after fleeing Pharaoh's palace, spent forty years in the Sinai tending goats before God finally called him back to demand the release of the Israelite slaves. David was anointed by Samuel to be the next king of Israel, but he went through twenty-five years and a whole lot of trouble before he finally assumed the throne. And consider Jesus, who at the age of twelve knew he had a unique relationship with God, but there would be eighteen years of waiting before he was baptized and began his three-year public ministry.

Was God at work during Abraham's twenty-five years of waiting? Or Joseph's twenty years? Were Moses' forty years in the wilderness wasted? Or David's twenty-five years, much of it spent avoiding King Saul's efforts to kill him? And what of Jesus? Was his Father at work in Jesus' life during those eighteen years when he labored alongside his earthly father?

In Paul's case, he spent ten years wondering what Ananias could possibly have meant and why he still was making tents when there was a big world out there to be saved. Perhaps his sense of calling began to fade during that time. But God was at work during the "in-between" time.

How often this pattern has persisted for those whom God uses to change the world. I think of John Wesley, who spent most of his twenties and thirties striving to do God's will but often feeling like a failure. Finally, after his greatest disappointment, God unleashed him to lead a revival across Great Britain that would leap across a continent and change the world.

Have you ever experienced an "in-between time"? Perhaps you are experiencing one now. God is at work, trust that! Keep putting one foot in front of the other! Moses, David, Jesus, Paul, Wesley, and many others did not stop dreaming, thinking, and working as they waited, and in the waiting God was preparing them, transforming them, and readying them for what lay in store.

The Gospel Unleashed in Syrian Antioch

In Acts 11, Luke takes us to Antioch in Syria, also known as Antioch on the Orontes River. (There were at least sixteen cities named Antioch in Asia Minor and Syria, two of which play an important role in Paul's story.) Syrian Antioch, known as the Crown of the Orient, was the third-largest city in the Roman Empire during Paul's time, with as many two hundred fifty thousand residents.*

Today the city is part of southeastern Turkey, twelve miles from the Syrian border, but in biblical times it was part of the Roman province of Syria. Most of the ruins from the time of Paul have yet to be excavated, but one site dates back at least to the 300s, with tradition dating the Cave Church of St. Peter to the time of Paul. According to that tradition, on a visit to Antioch, Peter found a cave or perhaps helped to carve one, where the first Christian community began to meet. The façade of the church dates to the 1800s, but the earliest portions of the building may date back to the 300s if not before.

* Just a reminder that population numbers are estimates and vary greatly depending upon the source.

This is the exterior and interior of the Cave Church of St. Peter in Syrian Antioch. Tradition says that Peter expanded the grotto so that the church at Antioch might meet there.

The ancient city of Syrian Antioch, located about three hundred fifty miles north of Jerusalem, was home to a relatively large Jewish population, and there were many Gentiles (non-Jews) who put their faith in God and sought to honor him by participating at the synagogues. Luke refers to these Gentiles as "God-fearers."

Apparently some of the followers of the Way had taken the gospel to Antioch, and Luke tells us that a "great number" of Jews and God-fearing Gentiles were becoming followers of Jesus. Luke reports in Acts 11:22 that "news of this came to the ears of the church in Jerusalem, and they sent Barnabas to Antioch."

This major metropolis, within the decade, would likely see the Christian community grow so rapidly that it became bigger than the church in Jerusalem, perhaps even than all the churches in the Holy Land. Antioch quickly became an important center of Christianity, and Luke tells us, it was here that the followers of Jesus first were called Christians.

Who Is Your Barnabas? Whose Barnabas Are You?

Before we conclude this chapter on Paul's conversion and early ministry, let's turn our attention to Barnabas, a man who would play a pivotal role in Paul's early ministry. We first read of Barnabas in Acts 4:36-37.

> There was a Levite, a native of Cyprus, Joseph, to whom the apostles gave the name Barnabas (which means "son of encouragement"). He sold a field that belonged to him, then brought the money, and laid it at the apostles' feet.

We learn a number of useful things in this short passage. We learn that Barnabas's given name was Joseph. We learn that, like Paul, he was a Jew of the Diaspora (a Jew who lived outside the Holy Land), from the island of Cyprus. We learn that he was a Levite. Levites, from the Israelite tribe of Levi, were assigned different roles during the history of Israel, but all were linked in some way to the priesthood, to the Tabernacle and later the Temple, and to the religious laws. Some Levites were priests. Some were musicians. Some were teachers, judges, even accountants. Levites maintained the Temple and the holy things of God. In the Diaspora, Levites were called upon to assist or read Scripture in the synagogue, a practice that is still observed in some synagogues today.

Barnabas appears to have been a devout Jew who had come to faith in Christ while in Jerusalem, quite possibly having heard Jesus speak or having been a witness to the Resurrection. Perhaps he was among the three thousand who came to faith on the day of Pentecost in response to Peter's preaching and the outpouring of the Holy Spirit.

We also learn in the passage from Acts 4 that Barnabas sold a field he owned and gave the proceeds to the apostles to be used to support their work and the needs of the believers in

Jerusalem.* He clearly was an extravagant giver. Jesus once said, "Where your treasure is, there your heart will be also" (Matthew 6:21). My experience with members of my congregation is that when people make a large gift such as this, it indicates the depth of their faith and commitment, or at the very least the act of giving deepens their faith and commitment.

Finally, we learn that the apostles gave him the name Barnabas, which Luke tells us means "son of encouragement," a magnificent name that undoubtedly described his character. We see his character, his habitual efforts at encouraging others, in Barnabas's interaction with Paul. In Acts 9:27, as we've already seen, Barnabas was the one leader in the Jerusalem church willing to take a chance on Paul when all others were afraid of him. Barnabas vouched for Paul and brought him to Peter and James. With Barnabas's vouching for him, the other disciples were willing to take a chance on Paul.

Now let's return to Antioch. At least ten years had passed since Barnabas had put Paul on a ship from Jerusalem to Tarsus in order to save Paul from those who wanted to kill him. Now, Barnabas had been sent by the apostles to see what the Spirit was doing among the new believers in Antioch. Luke reports:

> When [Barnabas] came and saw the grace of God, he rejoiced, and he exhorted them all to remain faithful to the Lord with steadfast devotion; for he was a good man, full of the Holy Spirit and of faith. (Acts 11:23-24)

I love this passage, both for the way Barnabas exhorted the new believers in Antioch and, particularly, for the words Luke uses to describe Barnabas: "He was a good man, full of the Holy Spirit and of faith." Would that each of us could be described

* There is some debate about whether Levites were forbidden from owning any real property by the Torah or whether they simply were not given a portion of the land as their inheritance during the conquest of Canaan and instead relied upon the tithes of the people. In any event, it appears from this text that some Levites in the New Testament period did own land.

by those words! In that one line there's a three-point sermon waiting to be proclaimed. There's a focus for an entire year's worth of prayers: "O Lord, make me like Barnabas, generous, an encourager, a good person. Fill me with your Holy Spirit, and with the gift of faith."

Luke goes on to tell us that Barnabas remained in Antioch leading the church, and "a great many people were brought to the Lord" (v. 24). In just these few short passages, Luke has painted a vivid picture for us of the kind of Christian Barnabas was—and the kind of Christian we might each seek to be—one who leads others to faith; the kind of leader who helps churches transform their communities, who shows kindness, who has a deep faith, who is led by and filled with the Holy Spirit.

As Barnabas saw what was happening among the Gentiles and Jews in the huge metropolis of Antioch, the New York City of the eastern Roman Empire, he remembered the educated and passionate young Pharisee he put on a boat for Tarsus some ten years earlier. Who do you think brought this thought to Barnabas's mind? My guess is the Holy Spirit. For many of us, when we have such thoughts we tend to dismiss them or fail to pay attention. But if, like Barnabas, we listen and pay attention, the Spirit can bring things to our minds that we've long forgotten. Luke tells us how Barnabas responded.

> Then Barnabas went to Tarsus to look for Saul, and when he had found him, he brought him to Antioch. So it was that for an entire year they met with the church and taught a great many people. (Acts 11:25-26)

Barnabas went on, as we will see in the next chapter, to travel with Paul on his first missionary journey. It is clear that at the start of the trip Barnabas was the more prominent of the two: Luke regularly refers to them as Barnabas and Saul. But at some point during that first missionary journey, Luke starts referring to them as Paul and Barnabas. Paul's star had risen; from that time on he received first billing. Barnabas seemed fine with this. In fact, I suspect he delighted in the fact that his protégé was coming into his own.

The last time we read about Barnabas is in Acts 15, when Paul and Barnabas had a disagreement and parted ways, something we'll discuss in a subsequent chapter. It's clear, though, that without Barnabas, Paul might have lived out his days making tents in Tarsus. It was Barnabas who believed in Paul when he first came to Jerusalem. It was Barnabas who introduced him to the apostles. It was Barnabas who found him during the in-between years and brought him to Antioch.

Barnabas never wrote a book of the Bible (though some have suggested he may have written the Letter to the Hebrews), but much of our New Testament would not exist without the encouragement he gave to Paul.

I wonder, do you have someone to encourage you? Do you have a Barnabas? Mine was a man named Bob Robertson. It was 1985. I had just graduated from college in Tulsa and had applied for a job as youth director at a United Methodist church in Dallas, since I was heading there to begin seminary in the fall at Southern Methodist University. I drove four hours to get to the interview, and when I arrived the church secretary told me, "Oh, our pastor decided to hire someone else. I'm sorry we forgot to let you know."

I had given up two days and spent what little cash I had on gas and a place to stay overnight. I left the church that day so very discouraged. I drove to the district office of The United Methodist Church and stopped to see if anyone there knew of any job openings. The secretary said, "I know someone who's looking for a youth director. His name is Bob Robertson." She called Bob, who invited me over. I drove to meet Bob at the church he was pastoring, New World United Methodist Church in Garland, Texas. On the spot he offered me a job. He saw something in me. Over the next three years he mentored me, encouraged me, and helped me believe in myself.

After I graduated from seminary, Bob regularly called or sent me notes of encouragement. He continued to believe in me and saw things in me I did not see in myself. I continue to thank God for the impact Bob had on my life, and I still wear a stole Bob's wife gave me after his death in 2002, one that reminds me of him and the role he played in my life.

One of the young people in my congregation collapsed at a football game because of a brain injury incurred on the field. He was comatose when I went to see him in the intensive care unit of the hospital, and his parents were not sure he would survive. When I stepped into the waiting room, I found his parents surrounded by friends, family, and fellow church members. We went to pray at their son's bedside in ICU. They said to me, "Pastor Adam, what has sustained us through this is the number of people who have come alongside us to encourage us. We could not have made it this far without them." As I write these words, their son is in rehab, steadily making progress toward recovery.

The young man and his parents needed encouragers. So do all of us. It's easy to be an encourager, and there's joy in it. Our task is to pay attention, looking for those who need our encouragement. That's what Barnabas did, and I can't help but wonder what would have happened to Saul of Tarsus without him.

All of us need a Barnabas. But it's important for us to remember that all of us are called to be someone else's Barnabas too. Part of our mission in life is to encourage others and to see in them what they may not see in themselves.

Who is your Barnabas? More importantly, whose Barnabas will you be?

2
Called to Go

Paul's First Missionary Journey

Now in the church at Antioch there were prophets and teachers: Barnabas, Simeon who was called Niger, Lucius of Cyrene, Manaen a member of the court of Herod the ruler, and Saul. While they were worshiping the Lord and fasting, the Holy Spirit said, "Set apart for me Barnabas and Saul for the work to which I have called them." Then after fasting and praying they laid their hands on them and sent them off. So, being sent out by the Holy Spirit, they went.

—Acts 13:1-4a

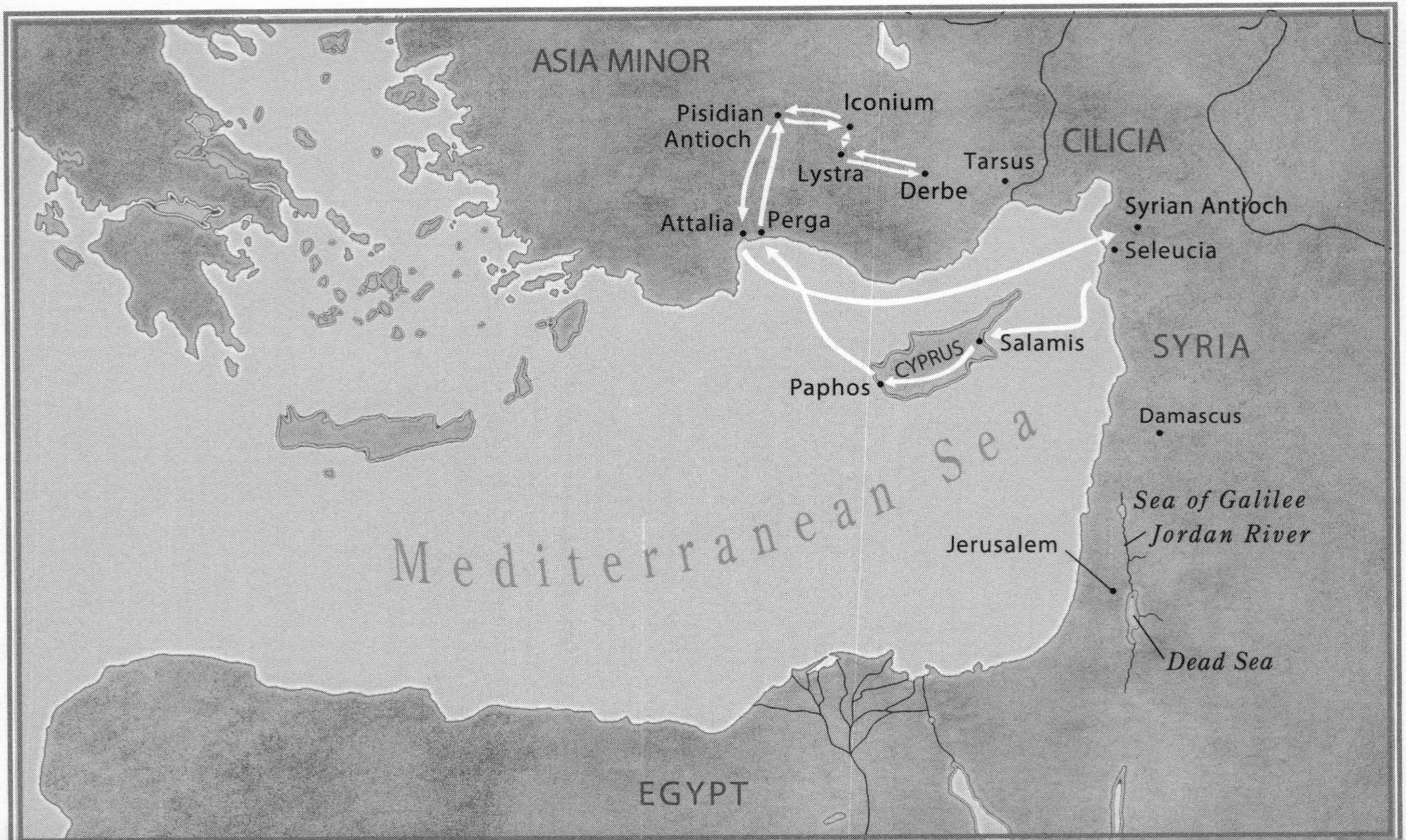

ASIA MINOR
Pisidian Antioch
Iconium
Lystra
Derbe
Tarsus
CILICIA
Attalia
Perga
Syrian Antioch
Seleucia
CYPRUS
Salamis
Paphos
SYRIA
Damascus
Mediterranean Sea
Sea of Galilee
Jordan River
Jerusalem
Dead Sea
EGYPT

A.D. 67 Paul's Death

65

60

55

50

A.D. 49-50 Paul writes Galatians?

A.D. 49-50 Paul and Barnabas return to Syrian Antioch

A.D. 49 Paul and Barnabas begin "first" missionary journey

A.D. 48 Paul and Barnabas to Jerusalem

A.D. 47 Barnabas to Syrian Antioch; with Paul at Tarsus

45

40

A.D. 38-48 Paul in Tarsus and region (est.)

A.D. 38 Paul meets Peter and James in Jerusalem

A.D. 35-38 Paul in Arabia, then Damascus

35

A.D. 35 Paul is converted on road to Damascus (est.)

A.D. 32 Paul arrests Jesus followers in Palestine (est.)

30

25

20

A.D. 16-22 Paul begins study in Jerusalem (est.)

15

5 B.C.-A.D. 10 Paul is born (est.)

5 B.C. - A.D. 10 Paul is Born (est.)

OFTEN GOD'S CALL SEEMS TO COME with no clear direction except "Go!" In our Google Maps world, having no clear direction can make us crazy. We want to know exactly where we're going before we start, along with step-by-step directions for how to get there. But God's direction for us is often less clear in the moment we are called. It requires us to pay attention at each step and sometimes to look for signs.

We'll see this again and again in Paul's major missionary journeys. When he set out, Paul counted on God to lead, not being completely clear precisely where God's Spirit would take him. He simply knew God was calling, and at every juncture he responded to that call.

Christians Aiding Other Christians

When we last saw Paul, Barnabas had sought him out during Paul's in-between years and had brought him to the church in Syrian Antioch, where they ministered to the Jewish and Gentile believers for a year.* During that year, a prophet named Agabus came from the church in Jerusalem to the church at Antioch predicting an imminent famine across the empire. In Acts 11, Luke tells us that this was when Claudius was emperor in Rome (from A.D. 41 to 54).

The famine is testified to by several Roman historians and appears to have occurred between 46 and 48, which fits our proposed timeline showing Paul's year in Antioch around 47.† Agabus may have given his prediction of the famine before

* This Antioch is typically called Syrian Antioch, as it was in the Roman province of Syria, but this is sometimes confusing for modern readers because today "Syrian" Antioch is located in southeastern Turkey, twelve miles from the Syrian border.

† I should point out that Paul's journey with Barnabas from Antioch to help the believers in Jerusalem is not mentioned by Paul in his letters, unless it's the same visit Paul mentions in Galatians 2:1-10. This is one of several places where the chronology of Paul's life as described in Acts is difficult to reconcile with Paul's own comments in Galatians and other epistles.

Paul's arrival, thus during the year that Paul was present in Antioch the hardships related to the famine would have begun to be felt in Jerusalem. Luke goes on in Acts 11 to record the disciples' decision to provide relief, according to their ability, to the believers living in Judea; this they did, sending it to the elders by Barnabas and Paul.

The relief provided by the Antioch church is the first time we read of Christians outside the Holy Land sending aid back to the believers there. The Antioch Christians likely included a large number of Gentiles; thus we find not only Jews but also Gentiles sending aid to the Jewish Christians in Jerusalem. Five to seven years later, during his third missionary journey, Paul would ask for something similar when he went to churches he had founded across modern-day Greece and Turkey, made up largely of Gentile believers, and asked for an offering to support the believers in Jerusalem who were in need of help. We don't know if this second act of compassion was in response to a famine or persecution or some other form of hardship in Jerusalem, though it is often assumed to be another famine. (We'll consider that offering and what Paul writes about it in Chapter 5.)

What is evident in both relief efforts is that Paul and the early Gentile Christians felt it was their responsibility to give aid to Jewish believers in Jerusalem. They felt called to help Christians in other parts of the world in their time of need. These offerings were both an act of compassion and a means of building bridges between Gentile and Jewish believers. They also point to a basic characteristic of believers in Jesus: generosity.

The calling of Christians with resources to help believers in other places became a pattern that churches followed for the next two thousand years. As I'm completing the revision to this chapter, I'm on my way back to the United States from Africa with a group of Christians from the church I serve. We were visiting Malawi, one of several countries where we've partnered with indigenous Methodist churches. On our first visit to Malawi four years ago, we flew into the city of Lilongwe and then drove for several hours into the bush to meet with tribal chiefs and leaders of small Christian communities. It was an amazing experience visiting with villagers, singing and worshiping and listening to the stories of what God was doing in their lives, churches, and communities.

During that first visit, a group of local leaders walked us to their water supply about a mile away from their village. It was a stream with brownish-green water that they used for drinking, cooking, and bathing. Village elders told us they prayed for clean water, water that would no longer make their children sick. In other villages we learned of other humanitarian needs, equally compelling. Thus began a four-year partnership that has our members traveling to Malawi, and Malawians traveling to our church. Malawian Christians have poured into us, and we into them. And together we were able to construct twenty deep-water wells, develop agricultural projects, and much more.

In Paul's second letter to the Corinthians, he discussed an offering for the believers in Jerusalem and noted the importance of striking a "fair balance between your present abundance and their need, so that their abundance may be for your need" (2 Corinthians 8:13-14). In all the mission work we pursue at the Church of the Resurrection, this is our aim: not doing mission work *to* others but partnering *with* others, so our abundance helps meet their need and their abundance meets ours. The Malawian Christians extended hospitality and welcomed our teams. They taught us about their community. They bore witness to their faith. They helped us grow in our own faith. They sang for us and celebrated with us. They came to the United States to work with our church's mission staff and help make us more effective. An intern from Malawi served on our staff for nearly a year. Ultimately our friends from Malawi enlarged the hearts of our congregation.

God's most common way of answering prayers is through people. But for that to work, Christians must pay attention and listen, we must put ourselves in a position to see others' needs, and we must respond when God calls. My return to Malawi was in part to celebrate what God has done through our partnership, but it was also to listen, pay attention, and seek to hear God's continuing call for our shared ministry.

God's Call in Worship and Fasting

Paul and Barnabas journeyed from Syrian Antioch to Jerusalem to deliver relief to the Jewish Christians. When they returned to Antioch, they brought with them a disciple named John Mark, whom Paul describes in Colossians 4:10 as the cousin of Barnabas. What happened on their return launched Paul on his career as a missionary to the Gentiles. Luke writes,

> While they [the believers in Syrian Antioch] were worshiping the Lord and fasting, the Holy Spirit said, "Set apart for me Barnabas and Saul for the work to which I have called them." Then after fasting and praying they laid their hands on them and sent them off. (Acts 13:2-3)

Model of the temple in Jerusalem as Paul and Barnabas would have seen it

Notice that it was in the context of worship and fasting that the Holy Spirit spoke to the believers, calling Barnabas and Saul (Paul) to go and do the work God had called them to do—taking the gospel to the world. Finally, more than a decade after his conversion, Paul was being given his marching orders by the Spirit through the church.

The book you hold in your hands is titled *The Call*. The title captures something important about Paul's life. His story is in so many ways the story of a man hearing God's call and responding. The title and the book are not meant simply to recount Paul's story, but to allow Paul's story to speak to our story—to help us listen for and hear God's call on our lives and to encourage the reader (and the author!) to respond. With that in mind, notice what Barnabas and Paul were doing when they heard God's call to embark on their mission to the Gentiles: Luke tells us they were "worshiping the Lord and fasting."

Among the times I am most likely to hear God speaking is when I'm with others in worship. I always bring a pen and paper to worship, whether I am at the Church of the Resurrection or attending church somewhere else. I expect that God will speak. I pray on my way to church, "Lord, please speak to me in worship today." When I'm preaching I pray, "Lord, speak through me to your people." As I sing, pray, listen to music, and particularly as I listen to the sermon or as I preach it, I will often have at least one or two moments when a thought comes into my mind, or drills down into my heart, about something I should do, someone I should reach out to, or some way I should live differently. I believe that these thoughts are usually the Spirit speaking.

It was in worship that I first began to understand who Jesus is and what he asks of us. It was in worship that I felt God calling me to be a pastor. It was in worship that I discovered a deep conviction about missions and acts of mercy and justice. It was in worship that I felt God calling me to start a new congregation. Of course, I feel God leading and guiding me in private times of prayer, in small groups, in reading Scripture, in taking long walks, and in a thousand other ways. But for me, nowhere do I hear God's call more often than in worship with others. Maybe that's true for you too.

The past few years have seen a trend away from participating in congregational worship. I read recently that several prominent and well-published Christian leaders no longer attend worship. Some have said that they get what they need in their own devotions, through their individual pursuit of spiritual disciplines, or in Christian conversation with others. Some have frankly admitted that the preaching and music are not great in most churches, and they often leave the service uninspired.

Thankfully this was not the approach of Paul and Barnabas regarding worship. Do you think the music was awesome at that small church in Antioch? There was no contemporary "praise and worship band" with hipster leaders. There was no amazing traditional worship choir singing with a hundred-rank organ. But at least there was great preaching, right? After all, Paul was one of their preachers! Not so fast. In 2 Corinthians 10:10, Paul notes what others said about his preaching: "His letters are severe and powerful, but in person he is weak and his speech is worth nothing" (CEB). Despite Paul's apparently unimpressive preaching and despite the simple singing of "psalms and hymns and spiritual songs" (Ephesians 5:19) likely unaccompanied by instruments, God's Spirit spoke when the people gathered for worship at Antioch.

Several years ago I worshiped in Italy at a small Catholic church that is hundreds of years old. I don't speak Italian, and my Latin is almost nonexistent, but in the midst of the music, the creed, the Lord's Prayer, the message, and even the Eucharist (in which as a Protestant I was not invited to participate), God spoke to me. More recently I worshiped in the Ozarks of Missouri at a Pentecostal church with fewer than twenty people, but God spoke to me in the midst of their spirited worship. Some people find that excellent music and preaching make it easier to hear God speak, but I find that moments of silence can be equally powerful. I believe the Spirit shows up "where two or three are gathered" in Christ's name (Matthew 18:20), in a way that we don't experience the Spirit's work anywhere else. Our task in worship is to prepare ourselves spiritually to hear the Spirit speak, sometimes despite the music and preaching.

Besides worshiping, the church in Antioch was fasting. It wasn't just that individual members were fasting, as important as this discipline can be in our spiritual lives, the church members were fasting together, seeking God in an intense way. There are several places in the Old Testament where leaders called the community to fast together as a way of seeking God's guidance, protection, or help. (See examples in 2 Chronicles 20:3, Ezra 8:21, and Esther 4:15-16.) Similarly, the church leaders at Antioch called their community to fast together, as they had worshiped together. It was through these acts of group devotion that Paul received his greatest call from God, one that would take the Way from being a small sect within Judaism to being the largest religion in the world.

In many congregations a bulletin is prepared to guide worshipers through the service, listing each hymn, prayer, and act of worship. But at the church I serve, our bulletin does not show the order of worship. It does not list the hymns or songs of praise. Instead, it's filled with information about mission and service opportunities. We assume that, as in the church at Antioch, the Spirit will call people to mission and service during our worship. We list opportunities for people to respond to the Spirit's call. Put another way, our bulletin is not meant to tell people what to do in worship; it invites them to consider what to do when they leave!

The Christians at Antioch, after worshiping and fasting together, heard the Spirit's call for Paul and Barnabas to pursue God's mission to the world. Hearing the call, the believers in Antioch laid their hands on Barnabas and Paul and sent them off.

The "First" Missionary Journey

And so we come to Paul and Barnabas's "first" missionary journey. I've used quotation marks around the word *first* because it's clear when we read Acts that Paul had made multiple journeys in mission for Christ before the so-called first missionary journey. He had proclaimed Christ in Damascus, likely in the desert near Damascus, in Tarsus and around Cilicia and Syria, and he had traveled to Jerusalem on a mission to deliver aid to the believers there. But the journey he and Barnabas were about to embark upon was different. Up to this point Paul had taken the gospel to familiar territory. He had grown up in Cilicia. It's probable he had traveled often in and through Syria. He had lived and studied in Judea. But now Paul would offer the good news wherever the Spirit led, including places where he had never been before.

As noted at the beginning of this chapter, when you read about Paul's missionary journeys in Acts, it seems clear that when he set out, he often did not have a clear idea exactly where he was going. I'm reminded of God's call upon Abraham and Sarah to "go from your country and your kindred and your father's house to the land that I will show you" (Genesis 12:1). God didn't say exactly where that land was, only that God would show them when they got there. This is not unlike the call many seminary students have answered. They have heard God calling them to full-time ministry, and they feel led to a particular seminary, but beyond that they have no idea where their lives and career will end up. They simply say, "Here I am Lord; send me." It is like many lay people who respond to a need or a call to serve without being completely certain what they are signing on for. Despite the lack of clarity, they say, "Lord, where you lead me, I will follow."

Barnabas and Paul* likely traveled along the Orontes River, the chief river in this part of Syria, which flowed to the Mediterranean Sea near the port city of Seleucia, some fifteen miles, as the crow flies, from Antioch.†

Luke mentions in passing (Acts 13:5b) that Barnabas and Paul were joined by young John Mark, who came to assist them. It's worth taking a moment to say a few words about this young man. In Acts 12:12 we read that Peter, upon his miraculous release from prison, "went to the house of Mary, the mother of John whose other name was Mark, where many had gathered and were praying." Mark and his mother were early followers of Jesus in Jerusalem, and their home was a gathering place for the church. Some have suggested that Mark was the anonymous young man who nearly had been arrested with Jesus in Mark 14:51-52 and that the author of the Gospel of Mark included this story as an autobiographical signature. As noted earlier, Colossians 4:10 tells us that John Mark was a cousin of Barnabas. John Mark was mentioned by Peter as "my son" and appeared to be with Peter in Rome in the early 60s, just before Peter's death (see 1 Peter 5:13). John Mark was later remembered by the early church as Peter's interpreter in Rome. Hence the Gospel of Mark is thought to be John Mark's account of what he had heard Peter tell of Jesus' life and ministry. Paul mentions Mark again (assuming this is the same Mark) in 2 Timothy and Philemon.

In any event, when Barnabas, Paul, and John Mark left on Paul's first missionary journey, they boarded a boat in Seleucia. The journey they were embarking upon would ultimately entail 1,580 miles of travel and take somewhere between six months

* At this point in Luke's account of their journey, Barnabas's name is almost always mentioned first, pointing to the authority and esteem he carried in the church. Be aware too that in Luke's account, Paul is still referred to by his Hebrew name, Saul.

† It is possible that these small boats would have been portaged at certain points.

The modern harbor at Antalya, near the ancient city of Perga

and a year.* The first stop on their journey was the island of Cyprus. We learn in Acts 4:36 that Barnabas was from Cyprus. You can read of their time on Cyprus in Acts 13:4-12, a visit of a week or two that ultimately resulted in the Cyprian governor converting to Christ.

From Cyprus, Barnabas and Saul, along with young John Mark, set sail for Perga on the south-central coast of modern Turkey. In Paul's day what we now call Turkey was known as Asia Minor ("little Asia") or Anatolia (signifying in Greek something like "the land where the sun rises"). This region consisted of numerous Roman provinces and geographic areas. Perga was within the area known as Pamphylia in southern Asia Minor.

---

* This distance was for Paul and Barnabas only; as we will see, John Mark would travel just a portion of the journey. The mileage total is taken from Stanford's Orbis site: http://www.openbible.info/blog/2012/07/calculating-the-time-and-cost-of-pauls-missionary-journeys/.

The ancient city of Perga lay about 165 miles northwest of Cyprus and seven miles inland from the Mediterranean Sea.* If Paul and his friends traveled by ship, their journey could have taken anywhere from two to six days, depending upon the winds.† Some ancient sources say that ships could travel up the Cestrus River to Perga, though today the river is more a shallow stream. Whatever method Barnabas, Paul, and John Mark used, Luke tells us they came to Perga upon arriving in Asia Minor.

Two things in Acts are worth noting. In his account of the trip, Luke makes a noticeable shift in how he refers to Paul. Previously he had used the Hebrew name Saul, but after the conversion of the governor of Cyprus, Luke always uses the Roman name Paul. And while up to this point he had referred to "Barnabas and Saul," he now starts referring to them as Paul and Barnabas, or simply as "Paul and his companions" (13:13). The difference in terminology is small, but it seems to indicate, based upon what follows, that Paul has taken on leadership of the mission to the Gentiles.

Have you ever had someone you trained and mentored at work, perhaps a new employee, who after several years was promoted to become your boss? Some people are able to handle this. The most gracious of us (and often older and wiser of us) actually celebrates the success of our younger protégés.

* Regarding distances cited in this book, where possible I used Google Earth, finding the archaeological ruins by means of the satellite images and then employing the measuring feature to determine distances. Interestingly this method sometimes yielded very different measurements from some of the excellent books about Paul that were written in the days before such Internet resources were available. For instance, measuring from the ruins at Perga to the closest shoreline of the Mediterranean Sea in Google Earth yielded a distance of 7.5 miles, but in books the distance is often cited as 6 miles. Between any two sources, distances often differ. All of which is to say that distances in this book will always be approximate.

† My estimate allows for some tacking back and forth, which would have extended the total miles traveled. Without tacking, the estimate would be one to four days. To see how I arrived at these numbers see Lionel Casson, "Speed Under Sail of Ancient Ships," Transactions of the American Philological Association, no. 82 (1951):136–148, reproduced online at http://penelope.uchicago.edu/Thayer/E/Journals/TAPA/82/Speed_under_Sail_of_Ancient_Ships*.html.

This is part of the "nymphaeum," a beautiful water feature that ran through the center of the main street in ancient Perga.

Barnabas, who had mentored and encouraged Paul for years, seems to have accepted this new leading role for Paul.

But upon arriving in Perga, young John Mark may have struggled a bit with the new arrangement. Luke tells us in that same passage that "John . . . left them and returned to Jerusalem." John's leaving appears to have been the source of a later falling out between Paul and Barnabas that would keep them from ever traveling together again.

Following in Paul's Footsteps

In the summer of 2014 I flew into the city of Antalya with a small film crew to retrace Paul's missionary journeys, starting with his visit to Perga, located just a few miles northeast of Antalya. We spent the next two weeks traveling across Turkey, Greece, and Italy, visiting archaeological sites associated with Paul's travels on his first, second, and third missionary journeys and his final journey to Rome.

Regarding Perga, our first stop, Luke has little to say about Paul and Barnabas's ministry there. They seem to have only passed through, likely resting for the night, but nothing is said of their preaching there until their return visit, months later. Instead they seemed quickly to head into the beautiful mountains just north and east of Perga. Why didn't they stay in Perga and preach as they did nearly everywhere else?

Maybe my experience traveling to Perga offers a clue. We arrived in Perga in August. The city is bounded by mountains to the north, west, and east, and the ocean to the south. Being several miles inland, Perga doesn't benefit from the cooling effect of the ocean, so the weather is stifling. We toured the archaeological remains of the city and tried filming, but I kept having to stop and wipe my brow. The temperature was in the nineties, but the humidity was what made it unbearable.

Based on our experience, it seems quite possible that Paul found the heat as unbearable as we did. Even so, would the heat have kept him from staying a few days to preach? Probably not. Yet he seemed in a hurry to head into the mountains and the high plains, where the humidity and temperatures are more comfortable. Many have suggested that Paul's reason for the quick departure was that he was sick.

Paul's letter to the Galatians was likely written following this first missionary journey and specifically to the churches that Paul would found after passing to the other side of the mountain range from Perga.* Paul wrote, "You know that it was because of a physical infirmity that I first announced the gospel to you" (Galatians 4:13). What was the physical infirmity Paul is talking about here?

Some believe it was malaria, a common illness contracted throughout the coastal regions of the Mediterranean in the first century. Malaria brings with it headaches, vomiting, fevers, and

---

* There are several theories as to when Galatians was written and to whom. I subscribe to what is called the "South Galatian Theory." Under this theory, Paul is writing to the Galatian churches he started on the first missionary journey. He is writing to these churches from Syrian Antioch upon his return to that city following this journey, which would make Galatians the earliest of Paul's letters.

chills. These symptoms certainly would be enough to lead a person to seek cooler and less humid temperatures.

Others have suggested that Paul may have contracted trachoma, the leading cause of blindness in the developing world today. Trachoma is a painful infection of the eye with symptoms that include discharge in the eyes, swelling of the eyelids, and increased heart rate. Blindness can result after numerous infections.

Trachoma seems at least possible because Paul notes in Galatians 4:15, just two verses after mentioning the illness, that "I testify that, had it been possible, you would have torn out your eyes and given them to me." Later he closes the letter in Galatians 6:11 with these words: "See what large letters I make when I am writing in my own hand." This is considered by some to be evidence that Paul's eyesight was failing.

Whether suffering from malaria, trachoma, or some other illness, it appears that Paul was sick when he arrived in Perga. Yet he refused to turn back and go home with John Mark. Instead he began hiking north, ascending the mountains to take the gospel into the heart of Asia Minor, to the region of Galatia. I am reminded of one important attribute of Paul, or for that matter of anyone whose actions change the world: perseverance. Paul refused to give up in the face of hardship.

Paul and Barnabas began their journey north into the mountains, heading toward a city we know as Pisidian Antioch, not to be confused with Syrian Antioch, the city where their church was located. In Paul's time there were two roads they might have taken to Pisidian Antioch. There was a recently completed highway, the Via Sebaste (*Sebaste* is the Greek equivalent for the Latin *Augustus*—both relating to majestic or exalted), a road dedicated to the memory of the late emperor. This road was the better and safer of the two, but it would have taken Paul and Barnabas to the west, forty miles out of their way. An alternative route was more direct, heading north from Perga. It was more primitive, difficult, and yet direct.

This lake, nestled in the Taurus Mountains, was on the road from Perga to Pisidian Antioch.

We chose to travel the second road on our journey from Perga to Pisidian Antioch, figuring that it was likely Paul may have taken the more direct route. However, in this case the term *direct* may be a misnomer. As the crow flies, the distance from Perga to Pisidian Antioch is just over 90 miles. But with all the turns and switchbacks the modern road takes, the actual distance is about 120 miles. It took us nearly five hours, but that included a stop for Turkish coffee at the Karacaoren reservoir and several places where we got out of the van and went on foot, imagining Paul and Barnabas walking through those same mountains.

The scenery was breathtaking. Mountains tower over eight thousand feet above sea level, with beautiful evergreen forests all around and streams flowing along the side of the road. The area looks more like Colorado than anything I had ever imagined to see in Turkey. The mountains, part of the Taurus range, run along much of the southern coast of Turkey.

For Paul, traveling on the ancient roads would have included going up and down mountains, moving through passes, ascending and descending switchbacks, and crossing rivers. For us, it meant encountering herds of goats that stopped traffic and occasionally seeing Turkish men and women wearing traditional Turkish garb walking or herding. From our vantage point, we could look down into the valley and, from time to time, make out portions of the ancient roadways. The sight brought home the astonishing and humbling thought that Paul and Barnabas had seen these same sights as they traveled together nearly two thousand years ago.

Pisidian Antioch

The trip to Pisidian Antioch might have taken Paul and Barnabas as few as five days, but if Paul was ill it may have been more like a couple of weeks. Walking and driving the route reminded me of how much is missing from the biblical account of Paul's life. What Luke tells us in one verse—that Paul and Barnabas went from Perga to Pisidian Antioch—probably took them fourteen days, camping by the side of the road, hiking up and down mountains, all to take the gospel further into Asia Minor than it had likely gone before.

The last part of their trip would have taken them into what is known today as the Lakes Region of Turkey. They probably would have journeyed, as we did, along the shore of Lake Egirdir, one of the largest freshwater lakes in Turkey. It is a beautiful lake used for recreation during the summer and is only a few miles from one of Turkey's ski resorts.

Finally, Paul and Barnabas would have arrived in Pisidian Antioch, just northeast of the current city of Yalvaç. This Antioch, one of a number of cities in Syria and Asia Minor by that name, was not technically in the region of Pisidia but near it. The River Anthius flows nearby. As many as fifty thousand people lived there, and in Paul's day it was an important city in the region.

There were only a handful of visitors the day we arrived at the archaeological site in Antioch. In the distance behind us

The Lakes Region in central Turkey on the way to Pisidian Antioch

were the mountains we had passed through, and we stood on the Anatolian highlands plain, where native grasses covered the gently rolling hills surrounding the ruins. Archaeologists were working that day, carefully excavating a section of the city that remained hidden under prairie grasses.

We entered the site through one of the gates of the ancient city, then walked down one of the ancient main streets, its well-preserved roadway a testimony to the Roman civil engineers. In Paul's day, both sides of the street were lined with small shops and cafes. After passing the shops, visitors can climb the remains of the city's theatre, sitting down to imagine performances that once took place upon its stage. At one time the theatre seated fifteen thousand people.

Passing the theatre and continuing toward the high point of the city, those who lived in or were visiting the Antioch of Paul's day would have come to a triple arched gate, a *propylon*, which led into a massive courtyard and ultimately to a temple dedicated to Emperor Augustus. On the walls of this gate was engraved a document called the *Res Gestae Divi Augustus*, the Deeds of the Divine Augustus. The Roman emperor Augustus, who had died thirty-five years earlier, had written the document some years before his death and revised it multiple times. Across the course of its thirty-five paragraphs, Augustus, feigning humility, outlined his greatness. The words were to be engraved in stone or bronze throughout the empire. Sections of the *Res Gestae* from the propylon of Antioch can still be seen in the museum at the nearby city of Yalvaç.

Not long before Paul and Barnabas's arrival in the town, the massive temple had been constructed in the back of the courtyard dedicated to the newly deceased and deified emperor. The building was the tallest structure in ancient Antioch and towered over the rest of the city. The remains of this temple can still be seen today. Here the citizens of Antioch and the surrounding region demonstrated their loyalty to the empire by their offerings. Hymns were composed to the emperor. The emperor's titles, most of which he assumed while he was alive, were later claimed by his successors. These titles included Lord, Savior of the World, Pontifex Maximus (high priest), King of Kings, and Divine Son of a God. It is important to understand that these titles, used by Romans for the emperor, came to be

These are artist's renderings of the Temple to Augustus that once stood in Antioch, built not long before Paul arrived there. Only a portion remains of the temple ruins.

used of Jesus. This information about Augustus served as a backdrop for the preaching of the apostles as they pursued their mission to the Gentiles of the Roman Empire.

Paul's Sermon in Antioch

Luke tells us in Acts 13:14 that Paul and Barnabas arrived in Antioch. It seems likely that they arrived in town several days before the Sabbath, during which time they became familiar with the city.

> And on the sabbath day they went into the synagogue and sat down. After the reading of the law and the prophets, the officials of the synagogue sent them a message, saying, "Brothers, if you have any word of exhortation for the people, give it." (Acts 13:14-15)

Paul stood, gestured with his hand, and started to talk. What follows in Acts is the longest recorded sermon from Paul that we have in the New Testament.

What Paul did in Antioch became his *modus operandi*. He entered a town and began teaching in the synagogue. When the Jewish communities gathered in the synagogue, there almost always were some Gentiles who joined them for prayer and exhortation, Gentiles who were drawn to the monotheistic Jewish faith with its emphasis on a God of justice and love who created all things and ruled as King of the universe. As we learned in the previous chapter, the New Testament refers to these Gentiles as "God-worshipers" or "God-fearers." Such persons were included among the people of the synagogue and the Jewish community, to a point. It was only as the men underwent circumcision and possibly a form of baptism—a ritual bathing—that they became full converts; until then they seem to have been welcomed and yet retained a lesser status. It was these Gentile God-worshipers who found the gospel Paul preached to be so compelling.

Paul's message in the synagogue at Antioch began by recounting Israel's story, a story that each person in the synagogue would have known by heart. Then he proclaimed that Jesus was the long-awaited Savior from God, but he added that the leadership in Jerusalem had not recognized this and instead condemned him to die. Their actions, Paul noted, fulfilled the words of the prophets. Paul proclaimed that Jesus was crucified, dead, and buried, "But God raised him from the dead!" (Acts 13:30).

Paul concluded his sermon with these (and other) words:

> Let it be known to you therefore, my brothers, that through this man forgiveness of sins is proclaimed to you; by this Jesus everyone who believes is set free from all those sins from which you could not be freed by the law of Moses.
>
> (Acts 13:38-39)

I like the way Eugene Peterson captures this last sentence in *The Message*: "Everyone who believes in this raised-up Jesus is declared good and right and whole before God." Let's consider the meaning of the gospel Paul proclaimed.

According to Paul, the fundamental problem with the human condition is sin. Paul uses the word fifty-two times in his letters. The Greek word he used, *hamartia*, means literally to miss the mark. A similar Hebrew word for sin that is often used in the Old Testament means to stray from the path, which assumes there is a path we're meant to walk on.

Paul uses *hamartia* several different ways. It is first an orientation of the human soul. We have a tendency to stray from God's path, to miss God's target for our lives. We don't like rules. We don't want to be told what we can do or cannot do. If the speed limit is fifty-five, I want to drive sixty-five. If there is a sign saying "Do not touch," I suddenly have the desire to touch. If there is something I'm supposed to do, often I dread doing it. In his letter to the Romans, Paul puts it this way: "I do not understand my own actions. For I do not do what I want, but I do the very thing I hate.... I do not do the good I want, but the evil I do not want is what I do" (Romans 7:15, 19).

So sin is an orientation. But for Paul, sin is also an external influence that lures us away from God's path, as he writes in Ephesians 6:12: "For our struggle is not against enemies of blood and flesh, but against the rulers, against the authorities, against the cosmic powers of this present darkness, against the spiritual forces of evil in the heavenly places."

Sin is an orientation or human tendency, and it is an external influence. It is also, according to Paul, every act in which we turn, intentionally or unintentionally, away from God's will for human life. We're called to forgive, but we harbor resentment. We're called to faithfulness, yet we struggle with desire for our neighbor's spouse. We're called to show kindness, yet how easily we speak harsh words and practice selfish deeds. Tens of thousands go to bed hungry, yet many of us are overweight.

Nearly all the problems plaguing humanity today have sin at their root. Injustice, racism, the lure for and misuse of power, war, totalitarianism, materialism, infidelity, abuse, addiction, and so many more problems are caused by straying from God's path—they are all *hamartia*. Paul famously notes in Romans 3:23 that "all have sinned and fall short of the glory of God."

The condition of sin separates us from one another and from God. It harms our relationships, brings pain to our world, and leaves us alienated from God. Paul preached that Jews and Gentiles needed a savior—not a savior to deliver the Jews from the Romans, for as long as there is sin in the world there will be conquering and occupying powers; nor a savior like Caesar, who would enforce Rome's peace by the power of her legions and with the threat of utter destruction. What human beings need is a Savior who could save them from themselves.

Jesus the Savior

Jesus, Paul proclaimed, came to save us. He came to deliver us from sin, to win forgiveness for us, to call us to a new way of life, to change our hearts and minds, and then to deliver us from death and to eternal life. He came to call humanity to be a part of God's empire, which Jesus called the Kingdom of God.

It would require another book far longer than this one to completely unpack the ways in which Paul, in his sermon that day and in his letters afterward, speaks of Christ's saving work. Paul draws upon the metaphors and philosophical, theological, and social categories and images of his time to explain salvation and how it is brought about by Christ.

At times this or that assertion seems to contradict another assertion he makes with equal force elsewhere, sometimes in the same letter. In fact, the more literally and woodenly we read his metaphors, often the harder it is to make sense of them. I've studied Paul my whole adult life, read every word attributed to him multiple times, and read dozens of books about him, yet I freely admit there are times when I don't understand what he was saying. I've found it helpful to think of his *soteriology*—his way of talking about salvation—as being more like poetry than economics. He uses images and metaphors, all of which convey something important but each of which breaks down when pushed too far or when held in isolation.

Stepping back from all the details and metaphors, I think Paul's teaching about salvation can be summarized in a few big ideas. The fundamental idea is that Jesus, by his life, teachings, death, and resurrection, saves us from the fundamental existential problems we have as human beings: sin, alienation, hopelessness, fear, and death.

Another important idea, clearly recognized by Paul, is that the teaching of Jesus would have profound implications for Judaism. He understood that Jesus was initiating a new covenant, or binding agreement, between God and humanity. In Scripture we read of several previous covenants God had made with his people. In the most sweeping of these covenants, God gave the Israelites 613 laws, and if the laws were kept, God would be Israel's God and Israel would be God's covenant people. Recognizing that it was unlikely Israel could keep all the laws, God made provision for atoning for sin through a system of sacrifices. In contrast, Paul proclaims that Jesus initiated a new covenant, not only with Israel but also with the whole human race. Henceforth God would offer salvation to all who put their trust in Christ, who had become an atoning sacrifice for the entire human race. Our task, using this metaphor of atonement, is to accept Jesus' sacrifice for us and on our behalf.

We'll come back to this idea later. For now I'll simply return to this marvelous line from *The Message* in Paul's sermon to the people of Antioch that day as he preached in the synagogue there for the first time: "Everyone who believes in this raised-up Jesus is declared good and right and whole before God."

Do you feel the power of this message? Think of it—as you put your trust in the crucified and resurrected King, you are declared acceptable, good, right, and whole! It doesn't matter what anyone else has said about you. It doesn't matter that you've done things in the past that leave you feeling bad or unclean or ashamed before God. For Jesus, by his death and resurrection, has declared that you are good, right, and whole before God! It is Jesus, the Savior, the King, the Lord, the High Priest, who offers this salvation. The salvation came at a great cost to Jesus, but we can access it freely, simply by trusting in him and seeking to become his followers.

There's far more that can and should be said about Paul's gospel, and we'll return to it in subsequent chapters, but his preaching about salvation is a good start. In Acts 13:42-43, Luke goes on to tell us how the people responded to Paul's message that day in Pisidian Antioch.

> As Paul and Barnabas were going out, the people urged them to speak about these things again the next sabbath. When the meeting of the synagogue broke up, many Jews and devout converts to Judaism followed Paul and Barnabas, who spoke to them and urged them to continue in the grace of God.

The Developing Opposition

Luke tells us, "The next sabbath almost the whole city gathered to hear the word of the Lord. But when the Jews saw the crowds, they were filled with jealousy; and blaspheming, they contradicted what was spoken by Paul" (Acts 13:44-45). Keep in mind, as we learned earlier, that "the Jews" he speaks of are specifically those Jews who opposed the gospel, not all Jews. Paul and Barnabas were Jews. Many of those who would form the first church in Pisidian Antioch also were Jews. But there were some Jews who did not believe, and who were "overcome with jealousy."

Is it possible there were Jewish leaders who simply disagreed with Paul and Barnabas—some who did not believe their account of the resurrection, or some who felt their interpretation of Scripture did not make sense? Yes, I think there were faithful Jews who had good reasons for disagreeing with Paul and Barnabas. But it appears there were others whose disagreements were less principled and had to do more with jealousy than with beliefs.

We'll find that jealousy is a common response of some who opposed Paul. With that in mind, let's consider the emotion of jealousy for a moment and how, tragically, it can lead us astray. Imagine that you are a rabbi, and on a typical Sabbath seventy-five people show up for worship. Now imagine that a visiting rabbi arrives in town and you allow him or her to share greetings and a message with your congregation. Afterward, people in your congregation go on and on about what a wonderful speaker this visitor was. Then, the following week, over five hundred people come to hear the rabbi speak. Are you feeling a bit insecure yet? What if this person seems to know the Scriptures better than you do? How many times could you hear people rave about the visiting rabbi before it would start to bother you?

The older I get, the better control I have over my insecurities. I've come to hope that when I'm not preaching, the guest preachers, including our young associate pastors, will do an extraordinary job. We scheduled a guest preacher recently who was known to be an outstanding communicator. I told a pastor friend about the guest preacher, and my friend in a moment of candor said, "I'm not sure I'd want him preaching at my church. I'm afraid they'd want him to be their pastor. I've learned only to bring in guest preachers who are not as good at preaching as I am." When I was much younger I might have felt the same, but today I want excellent preachers filling the pulpit when I'm out. I celebrate when our congregation tells me what a terrific job they did.

This is not just an issue with preachers. I've seen it with men and women in the business world whose insecurities get the best of them as another employee outshines them. This insecurity can lead to gossip, backbiting, unpleasant office politics, and worse. I've seen it happen with school kids when a new student is better looking, stronger, or smarter than the current students.

In the case of the synagogue in Antioch, a handful of insecure Jewish leaders "incited the devout women of high standing and the leading men of the city, and stirred up persecution against Paul and Barnabas, and drove them out of their region" (Acts 13:50). But listen to Paul and Barnabas's response: "Because of the abundant presence of the Holy Spirit in their lives, the disciples were overflowing with happiness" (13:52 CEB). I love this! Despite the harassment given them by some of their fellow Jews, they overflowed with happiness! In fact, the disciples' joy will be a theme that we'll pick up again in the next chapter as we follow Paul's second missionary journey.

Paul and Barnabas left Antioch and took the Roman road, the Via Sebaste (the Way of Augustus), to Iconium. It was a seventy-mile journey as the crow flies, though much longer as they followed the road along the Taurus Mountains. Why would Paul use this route? It is possible Paul intended to take the Via Sebaste to where it met the road that led back to Tarsus, his hometown. Perhaps his initial plans were to follow the land route home, then back to Antioch in Syria.

Listen to what Luke says happened upon arriving in Iconium:

> Paul and Barnabas went into the Jewish synagogue and spoke in such a way that a great number of both Jews and Greeks became believers. But the unbelieving Jews stirred up the Gentiles and poisoned their minds against the brothers. So they remained for a long time, speaking boldly for the Lord. (Acts 14:1-3)

Notice that Paul and Barnabas kept preaching even after some tried to turn the new believers against them. This is a glimpse of something we'll see over and over again in Paul's character: perseverance. He refused to give up in the face of opposition. Without this trait, he never would have accomplished what he did. One of the key characteristics of people who change the world is that they rarely back down or give up.

Eventually Paul and Barnabas left Iconium when they learned that their detractors planned personal harm to them. But they would return within a few weeks, and Paul would return again on his second and third missionary journeys.

Iconium, where Paul and Barnabas traveled after leaving Pisidian Antioch

More Trouble

From Iconium, Paul and Barnabas traveled nearly twenty miles to Lystra. Luke tells us in Acts 14:8-18 that Paul saw a man who "had been crippled from birth." Paul said to the man, "Stand upright on your feet." The man stood and began to walk. This amazing recovery created quite a stir in the small village of Lystra. The people believed that the gods had come to visit them, and the priest at the temple of Zeus, located just outside the city, brought animals to be sacrificed to Paul and Barnabas.

Paul and Barnabas were mortified! They shouted to the crowd who had gathered to worship them.

> "Friends, why are you doing this? We are mortals just like you, and we bring you good news, that you should turn from these worthless things to the living God, who made the heaven and the earth and the sea and all that is in them. In past generations he allowed all the nations to follow their own ways; yet he has not left himself without a witness in doing good—giving you rains from heaven and fruitful seasons, and filling you with food and your hearts with joy." (14:15-17)

Paul's words to the people of Lystra foreshadowed a similar speech he would make in Athens on his second missionary journey. Paul contrasted the living God with "worthless things" such as the pagan gods. The word *worthless* might better be translated as *empty*, another meaning of the Greek word. The difference is subtle, but to my ear *worthless* sounds harsh. I don't think Paul intended to insult the Lystrians but instead was urging them to hear the good news he and Barnabas had come to offer.

Paul told them the living God was the one who had made the earth and all that was in it. God had allowed nations to go their own way, but he always had left a "witness"—the blessings he gave to all, including those who didn't know God: rain, seasonal harvests, food, and happiness. I find Paul's statement to be

The tell of Derbe. In ancient times, when a city was destroyed it was rebuilt atop the ruins of the previous city, forming a mound or "tell."

remarkable: even among those who did not know God, God sought to provide for them and to offer them happiness.

Then disaster struck, and it's not clear exactly how or why. Apparently some of the Jews who had opposed Paul and Barnabas in Antioch and Iconium arrived and "won the crowds over." Soon Paul, who had been hailed as a god just moments earlier, was being pummeled with stones until it appeared that he was dead. After his apparent death he was dragged outside the city walls.

In the midst of tragedy, we can't help seeing the irony. In many ways, Paul's conversion began with his giving approval for the stoning of Stephen. His life looked as if it had come to an end in the same way.

However, it appears that some who had come to faith in Antioch and Iconium had begun traveling with Paul and Barnabas, because Luke tells us that "the disciples" gathered around Paul's lifeless body. As they wept and prayed, suddenly he sat up! You can imagine the rejoicing among this small band of believers and the great relief they must have felt.

Then Luke delivers a line I love: "He got up and went into the city" (14:20). What does it tell us about Paul that just after being stoned nearly to death, he went back into the same city? If he wasn't foolish, he surely was courageous and persistent.

The next day, we are told, Paul left with Barnabas, traveling to Derbe, sixty-five miles, as the crow flies, to the east. Luke tells us only that Paul and Barnabas "proclaimed the good news to that city and had made many disciples" (14:21). Were they in Derbe for a week, two weeks, only a day or two? We don't know.

The Importance of Leaders in the Church

Paul and Barnabas left Derbe, but instead of continuing on to Tarsus they decided to return to the cities where they had just preached the gospel, cities where they had been stoned, harassed, and asked to leave—back to Lystra, Iconium, and Antioch.

Their decision to return to these cities was critical and strategic. Here is what they returned to do:

> They strengthened the souls of the disciples and encouraged them to continue in the faith, saying, "It is through many persecutions that we must enter the kingdom of God." And after they had appointed elders for them in each church, with prayer and fasting they entrusted them to the Lord in whom they had come to believe. (Acts 14:22-23)

What we see here is Paul organizing the disciples into churches and providing a structure for each church to continue after he left. This became an important part of the success Paul had in creating enduring communities of faith. Some decry "organized religion," but the truth is that it's generally only as believers organize that they become functioning communities and have a lasting impact. George Whitefield, a companion of John Wesley, famously noted the difference between Wesley's ministry and his own. Whitefield was likely the better preacher, but Wesley was the better organizer. Whitefield is reported to have acknowledged this when he observed that Wesley organized his converts into "classes" and "thus preserved the fruit of his labor. This I neglected, and my people are a rope of sand."*

Paul, from that point on, organized the converts he made into communities with "elders" charged with the responsibility of providing leadership. Years later, Paul or one of his disciples described the requirements and responsibilities of the elders in this way.†

> The reason I left you behind in Crete was to organize whatever needs to be done and to appoint elders in each city, as I told you. Elders should be without fault. They should be faithful to their spouse, and have faithful children who can't be accused of self-indulgence or rebelliousness. This is because supervisors [Paul uses the word *episcopai*, usually translated as bishop or overseer and, at least in Titus, used synonymously with elder] should be without fault as God's managers: they shouldn't be stubborn, irritable, addicted to alcohol, a bully, or greedy. Instead, they should show hospitality, love what is good, and be reasonable, ethical, godly, and self-controlled. They must pay attention to the reliable message as it has been taught to them so that they can encourage people with healthy instruction and refute those who speak against it.
>
> (Titus 1:5-9 CEB)

When I read that elders should have children who can't be accused of self-indulgence or rebelliousness, it always strikes me that only a man who never had children could have written

* The conversation between John Pool, an eighteenth-century Methodist preacher, and George Whitefield is found in *Anecdotes of the Wesleys: Illustrative of Their Character and Personal History by John Beaumont Wakely* (New York: Carlton & Lanahan, 1870), 142. It can be found online in Google Books.

† Most mainline scholars believe that Titus and 1 and 2 Timothy were written after the time of Paul by one who was a disciple of Paul, offering the kind of guidance and instruction Paul had given while he was alive.

this! Nevertheless, Paul and his successors understood the importance of having effective, committed leaders—elsewhere he calls them shepherds—to help the community and its believers grow.

Take a look again at the description of what a leader in the church should and should not be. Some traits seem unattainable; for example, who is completely without fault? Perhaps what Paul had in mind was for us to recognize our imperfections, confess them freely, and apologize when we are at fault. Paul notes that leaders are not to be stubborn—the New Revised Standard Version (NRSV) translates this as "arrogant." In what way are stubbornness and arrogance connected? The Common English Bible (CEB), quoted above, says leaders are not to be irritable, where the NRSV says they are not to be quick-tempered. Paul says that leaders must not be addicted to alcohol. (Paul does not call elders to refrain from drinking wine; he himself drank wine, which was a safer drink than water in the first century.) Elsewhere Paul calls believers to eschew drunkenness. In addition, leaders are not to be bullies nor greedy.

Paul goes on to outline the positive traits to be sought in church leaders: "They should show hospitality, love what is good, and be reasonable, ethical, godly, and self-controlled." In the original, the word used for "hospitality" is the Greek *philoxenon*—literally, to love strangers. The word used in "love what is good" is *philagathos*—literally, to love what is intrinsically good or virtuous. In addition, leaders should be reasonable, wise, and sensible. They should be known for doing what is right and just. They should be godly—the Greek word signifies holiness, striving to be like God. And finally, leaders should have self-control or inner strength, the strength to do what is right and to refrain from doing what is wrong. I have never met anyone who is and does all these things all the time. But Christian leaders—pastors and lay leaders—are meant to strive for these qualities and to exhibit some measure of them.

At the church I serve, we have high standards for our leaders, both volunteer and staff. We ask them to sign a leader's covenant laying out our expectations that those in leadership positions will set examples for the congregation in their spiritual and personal lives. The most important and effective way we lead is by example. I recall what one of my college professors said: "You can't lead people where you yourself are not going."

It's worth noting that the elders Paul and Barnabas set aside were not formally trained. They had not been to seminary. In fact, most of these people had only been believers for a matter of days or weeks. Previously they may have been leaders in the synagogue, or in their brief time with Paul they may have demonstrated some aptitude or a particularly earnest desire to serve.

Paul came to believe it was essential to help ordinary believers hear God's call upon their lives to exercise leadership in the church. The church in all its ministries and expressions is highly dependent upon leadership. It's still true today in Sunday school classes, youth group, children's ministry, mission service, ushering, and administration. Paul trusted that the Holy Spirit would equip and guide leaders. He knew that without them, the fledgling church didn't stand a chance.

After Paul and Barnabas set aside and trained leaders for the churches they started, Paul continued to encourage, mentor, and help those leaders and the flocks they served by writing epistles or letters. These documents, making up more than half our New Testament documents, enable all of us to benefit from Paul's mentoring, theology, wisdom, and leadership advice.

Heading for Home

The churches Paul visited on his first missionary journey were located, broadly speaking, in the region of Galatia, and some believe that Paul's earliest letter, and thus the first "book" of our New Testament, was Paul's Epistle to the Galatians, possibly written from Syrian Antioch within a year of his starting the churches at Pisidian Antioch, Iconium, Lystra, and Derbe.

After setting aside elders in the churches he had started, Paul crossed the Taurus Mountains and came once again to Perga, the city he had passed through quickly earlier in his journey, but this time he "proclaimed the word" to its people. He then traveled ten miles west to the port city of Attalia, where he and Barnabas set sail for their home church of Syrian Antioch.

It is hard to know exactly how long Paul and Barnabas had been gone, but it seems reasonable to assume they had left Syrian Antioch six to nine months earlier. They had likely covered a distance of over fifteen hundred miles.

Upon arriving back in Syrian Antioch, Luke notes,

> When they arrived, they called the church together and related all that God had done with them, and how he had opened a door of faith for the Gentiles. And they stayed there with the disciples for some time. (Acts 14:27-28)

When Paul had left on his first missionary journey, he had heard a call to "Go!" but may not have known much more about his mission. Now, months later, he had traveled to new places, embraced believers, preached about sin and salvation, met opposition, suffered violence, and trained leaders. With each new experience his mission had become clearer, shaping him into the inspired and inspiring evangelist we know today.

More travels were coming, and more trouble. But Paul, called and claimed by Christ, was ready.

3
Called to Suffer

Paul's Second Missionary Journey (1)

Paul and his companions traveled throughout the regions of Phrygia and Galatia because the Holy Spirit kept them from speaking the word in the province of Asia. When they approached the province of Mysia, they tried to enter the province of Bithynia, but the Spirit of Jesus wouldn't let them. Passing by Mysia, they went down to Troas instead. A vision of a man from Macedonia came to Paul during the night. He stood urging Paul, "Come over to Macedonia and help us!" Immediately after he saw the vision, we prepared to leave for the province of Macedonia, concluding that God had called us to proclaim the good news to them.

—Acts 16:6-10 CEB

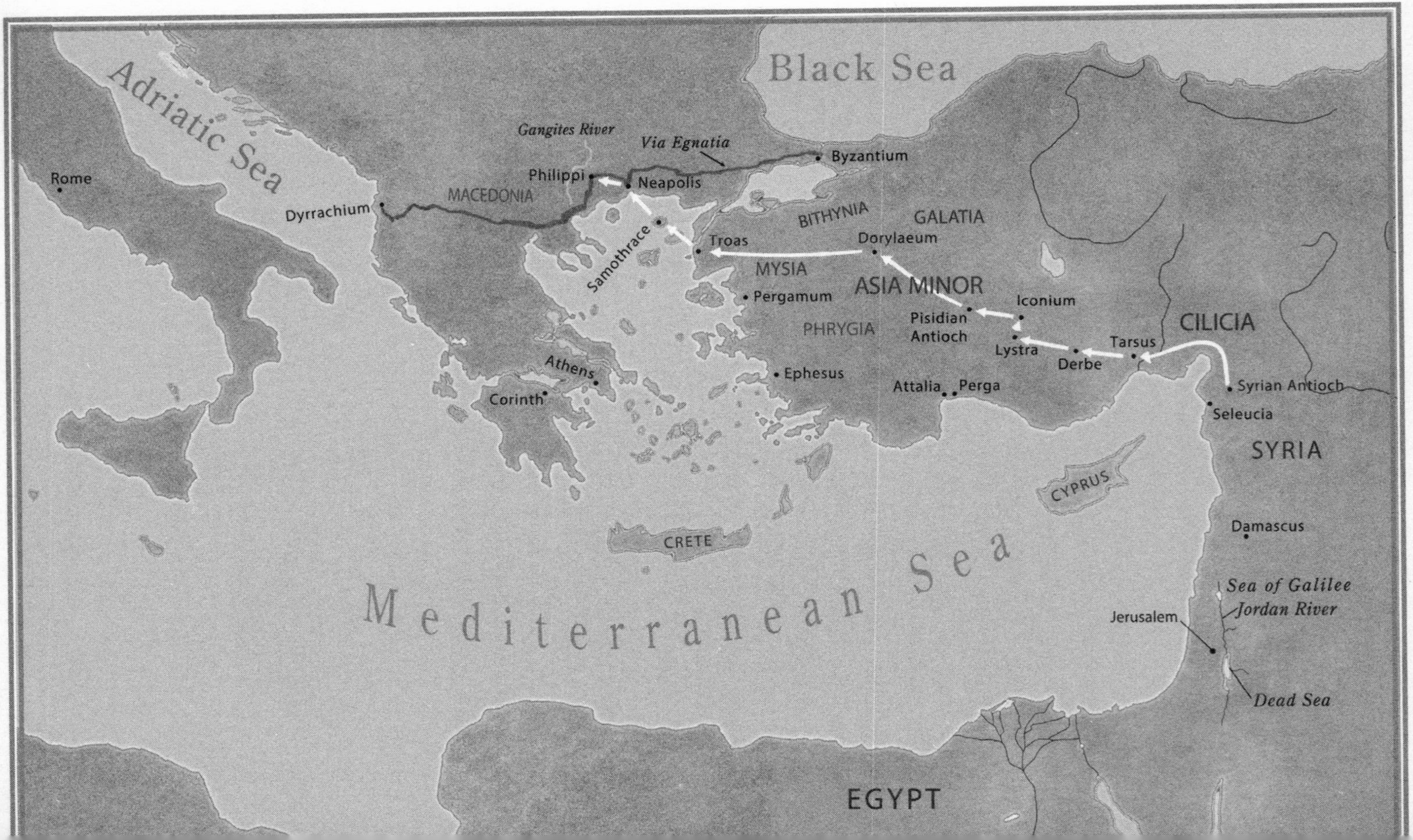

Black Sea
Adriatic Sea
Gangites River
Via Egnatia
Byzantium
Rome
Philippi
Neapolis
MACEDONIA
Dyrrachium
BITHYNIA
GALATIA
Dorylaeum
Troas
Samothrace
MYSIA
ASIA MINOR
Pergamum
Iconium
Pisidian Antioch
PHRYGIA
CILICIA
Tarsus
Lystra
Derbe
Athens
Ephesus
Attalia
Perga
Syrian Antioch
Corinth
Seleucia
SYRIA
CYPRUS
Damascus
CRETE
Mediterranean Sea
Sea of Galilee
Jordan River
Jerusalem
Dead Sea
EGYPT

A.D. 67 Paul's Death

65

60

55

A.D. 50-51 To Galatia, Macedonia, Achaia

A.D. 50 Paul and Silas begin second missionary journey

50

A.D. 50 Jerusalem Council

A.D. 50 Conflicts over circumcision

A.D. 49-50 Paul writes Galatians?

A.D. 49-50 Paul and Barnabas return to Syrian Antioch

A.D. 49 Paul and Barnabas begin "first" missionary journey

A.D. 48 Paul and Barnabas to Jerusalem

A.D. 47 Barnabas to Syrian Antioch; with Paul at Tarsus

45

40 A.D. 38-48 Paul in Tarsus and region (est.)

A.D. 38 Paul meets Peter and James in Jerusalem

A.D. 35-38 Paul in Arabia, then Damascus

35 A.D. 35 Paul is converted on road to Damascus (est.)

A.D. 32 Paul arrests Jesus followers in Palestine (est.)

30

25

20

A.D. 16-22 Paul begins study in Jerusalem (est.)

15

5 B.C. - A.D. 10 Paul is Born (est.)

5 B.C.-A.D. 10 Paul is born (est.)

PART OF WHAT I LOVE ABOUT READING Paul's letters and studying his life in Acts is that his humanity clearly shows through. Paul was a great leader, a remarkable theologian, and a courageous apostle. But he also was a human being. Like most of us, his greatest strengths could also be his greatest weaknesses. Paul's dogged determination meant that occasionally he was ungracious toward those with whom he disagreed. At times he lacked mercy toward those who disappointed him.

We'll see both those strengths and weaknesses in this chapter as Paul deals with disagreements among early followers of the Way, then sets out on his second missionary journey.

When we last saw Paul, he had just completed his first missionary journey and returned to his home church in Syrian Antioch. Upon arriving, he and Barnabas gathered the church together, reported the work God had done through them, and, according to Luke, "stayed with the disciples a long time." But soon they were faced with serious disagreements among believers with regard to Gentile converts.

> Some people came down from Judea teaching the family of believers, "Unless you are circumcised according to the custom we've received from Moses, you can't be saved." Paul and Barnabas took sides against these Judeans and argued strongly against their position. The church at Antioch appointed Paul, Barnabas, and several others from Antioch to go up to Jerusalem to set this question before the apostles and the elders. (Acts 15:1-2 CEB)

Division in the Ranks

This disagreement was the first major division within Christianity, one that would have far-reaching consequences. The church at Antioch was drawing an increasing number of Gentiles (non-Jews) who were choosing to become followers of Jesus Christ. Paul and Barnabas had just returned from a mission in which they formed several churches that were predominantly

Gentile. In both Antioch and those new churches, Gentiles were baptized but not circumcised, just as "God-fearers" in the synagogues had been allowed to worship with the Jews without being circumcised.

But if a Gentile man wished to fully convert and become a Jew, circumcision was required. It was seen as the outward and visible sign of the covenant between God and Abraham's descendants, as noted in God's words to Abraham:

> "You shall circumcise the flesh of your foreskins, and it shall be a sign of the covenant between me and you.... Any uncircumcised male who is not circumcised in the flesh of his foreskin shall be cut off from his people; he has broken my covenant." (Genesis 17:11, 14)*

The disciples who came from Judea were likely Pharisees who truly believed that Jesus was the Jewish Messiah. They did not cease to see themselves as Pharisees or Jews when they became followers of Jesus. In the first few decades following the death and resurrection of Jesus most believers were still Jews. Christianity was seen by many Jews as a sect within Judaism. It was at first suppressed but came to be tolerated. Jewish believers went to the temple, attended synagogue, met in one another's homes, and continued to follow the Law and oral traditions of first-century Judaism.

Jesus had not been afraid to challenge tradition in his teachings and actions. But it was Paul who taught that in Jesus' death and resurrection, the promise of God finally was fulfilled as prophesied in Jeremiah 31:31: "The days are surely coming, says the Lord, when I will make a new covenant with the house

---

* There are a number of theories as to why circumcision began to be practiced in ancient societies. The first known cases date to hundreds of years before the time of Abraham, among the Egyptians. In Paul's time, the Greco-Roman world derided the practice, believing the ideal male physique included the foreskin intact. Circumcision was a major hurdle to conversion to Judaism and Paul saw it as a nonessential barrier to full communion in the church.

of Israel and the house of Judah." Paul noted in 1 Corinthians 11:25 what Jesus himself had said as he took the cup at the Last Supper: "This cup is the new covenant in my blood." Paul had become convinced that Christ had initiated a new covenant between God and humanity. This covenant, or binding agreement between God and humanity, was not only for the Jew but also for the Gentile. It was a covenant that wasn't based on fulfilling the Law of Moses but on trusting Jesus Christ.

Paul believed that in Jesus Christ, God was offering salvation, grace, and right standing with him as a gift made possible by Jesus' death and resurrection. The gift was accepted by faith, not earned by obedience to the Law of Moses. Once accepted, the believer was to "lead a life worthy of the calling" (Ephesians 4:1), a life in which, led by the Spirit, he or she sought to love and honor God and love neighbor. Paul saw the Mosaic covenant as one made between God and Israel at a certain point in history and no longer binding upon either Jew or Gentile. Paul summarized his thinking in Romans 3:21-22 (CEB):

> But now God's righteousness has been revealed apart from the Law, which is confirmed by the Law and the Prophets. God's righteousness comes through the faithfulness of Jesus Christ for all who have faith in him. There's no distinction [between Jew and Gentile].

Armed with this understanding, Paul had preached to Jews and Gentiles during his recently completed missionary trip, saying they could receive salvation by trusting in Christ, that baptism was the sign of their new birth and washing by God, and that henceforth they would be God's people and should live to please him. Circumcision was not necessary. And while much in the Law might point to the kind of life God was asking his people to live, other portions were no longer relevant. In Christ there was no longer a division between Jews and God-fearing Gentiles. Instead, all were one in Christ.

Paul's view was compelling for Gentile God-fearers in the synagogues where he preached. His logic seems to have appealed to other Jewish followers of Jesus as well. But it is clear from Acts that not all Jewish followers of the Way agreed with Paul's theological convictions regarding circumcision and the Law—this seems particularly true of some among the believers in Jerusalem.

The Debate

This theological debate was behind four important events recorded in Acts and in Paul's letter to the Galatians, all of which seem to have occurred around A.D. 49–50 after Paul and Barnabas's return from the first missionary journey. We cannot be certain the timing or sequence of these events, but let's begin with a dramatic event that Paul records.*

> When Cephas [Peter] came to Antioch, I opposed him to his face, because he was wrong. He had been eating with the Gentiles before certain people came from James [the leader of the Jerusalem church]. But when they came, he began to back out and separate himself, because he was afraid of the people who promoted circumcision. And the rest of the Jews also joined him in this hypocrisy so that even Barnabas got carried away with them in their hypocrisy. But when I saw that they weren't acting consistently with the truth of the gospel, I said to Cephas in front of everyone, "If you, though you're a Jew, live like a Gentile and not like a Jew, how can you require the Gentiles to live like Jews?"

* For instance, in Galatians 2 Paul describes a trip to Jerusalem with Barnabas and Titus in which James, Peter, and John recognized Paul and Barnabas's ministry to the Gentiles. This almost sounds like what happens in Acts 15 at the council at Jerusalem, but in Galatians, following this visit to Jerusalem, certain people came from James in Jerusalem teaching that Gentiles needed to be circumcised. This would indicate that the visit described by Paul must have been before the Jerusalem Council of Acts 15.

Orontes River in Syrian Antioch

> We are born Jews—we're not Gentile sinners. However, we know that a person isn't made righteous by the works of the Law but rather through the faithfulness of Jesus Christ. We ourselves believed in Christ Jesus so that we could be made righteous by the faithfulness of Christ and not by the works of the Law—because no one will be made righteous by the works of the Law. (Galatians 2:11-16 [CEB])

In this passage Paul points out that Peter and other Jews ate freely with Gentiles until "certain people"—Jewish disciples sent by James—came to Antioch.* These Jewish disciples who came from James would appear to be the same persons described in Acts 15:1, quoted earlier: "Some people came down from Judea teaching the family of believers, 'Unless you are circumcised according to the custom we've received from Moses, you can't be saved'" (CEB).

In Paul's letter, he describes publicly confronting Peter. This was a surprising act, given the importance and prominence of

* This James was not the disciple James, but James who is called the "the Lord's brother." (See Galatians 1:19 and Mark 6:3.) Catholics note that the word *brother* in Greek can also signify a close relative who is not in the immediate family. They suggest that when James is referred to as the Lord's brother, it had this latter meaning.

Peter in the early church. It demonstrates Paul's *chutzpah*, as well as the strength of his convictions that no one is saved by the Law, that not even the Jews completely fulfill the Law, and that faith in Christ—not adherence to the Law—brings right standing with God. To treat the Gentiles as second-class or unclean is to violate the very essence of the gospel as Paul sees it.

Around this same time, it appears, some Jewish believers holding the same convictions as the group troubling the church in Antioch traveled to the Galatia region of Asia Minor, visiting the churches Paul and Barnabas had founded there and teaching these new Christians that they must be circumcised and must obey the Law. The new Christians were confused, and apparently some agreed to be circumcised and began following the Law of Moses. This prompted Paul to write his letter to the churches of the Galatia region: Antioch, Iconium, Lystra, and Derbe. Reading the letter today, we can feel Paul's anger and frustration at the Jewish believers who had confused the Galatian Christians. Paul writes to his converts in Galatia,

> I am astonished that you are so quickly deserting the one who called you in the grace of Christ and are turning to a different gospel—not that there is another gospel, but there are some who are confusing you and want to pervert the gospel of Christ. But even if we or an angel from heaven should proclaim to you a gospel contrary to what we proclaimed to you, let that one be accursed! As we have said before, so now I repeat, if anyone proclaims to you a gospel contrary to what you received, let that one be accursed! (Galatians 1:6-9)

The Greek word for accursed that Paul uses in this passage is *anathema*. The passage again shows the power of Paul's conviction that Christ initiated a new covenant—a new way of salvation that tore down the old wall between Jews and Gentiles, offering full acceptance and not second-class status to the uncircumcised Gentiles. This gospel that Paul preached offered salvation through faith in Jesus Christ.

Meanwhile, in Antioch, Paul publicly confronted not only Peter but also the believers who came from Judea teaching that Gentiles must be circumcised. Luke tells us,

> And after Paul and Barnabas had no small dissension and debate with them, Paul and Barnabas and some of the others were appointed to go up to Jerusalem to discuss this question with the apostles and the elders. (Acts 15:2)

When Paul and Barnabas arrived in Jerusalem, a gathering was held, a meeting usually referred to as the Jerusalem Council, at which the apostles and leaders of the Jerusalem church would decide the question of whether Gentiles must be circumcised and obey the Law of Moses. The council seems patterned after the Jewish Sanhedrin, which also met in Jerusalem. We don't know who the Christian elders were, but the practice of making key decisions by council became the pattern the church would follow for the next two millennia.

The Pharisees in the Jerusalem church had already made clear their position that Gentile Christians must be circumcised and required to keep the Law of Moses. The council was convened and much debate ensued. Finally Peter stood and offered his opinion that Gentiles should not be required to be circumcised or obey the Law. Then Paul and Barnabas testified to what God had done among the Gentiles in their ministry. Finally James stood and gave this judgment:

> "Therefore I have reached the decision that we should not trouble those Gentiles who are turning to God, but we should write to them to abstain only from things polluted by idols and from fornication and from whatever has been strangled and from blood." (Acts 15:19-20)

James's judgment, with its freedom from circumcision and from obeying the Law of Moses, was only for the Gentiles. Jews, presumably, were still required to obey the Law. There was within Judaism of this period an understanding among many that Gentiles could be righteous without following the Law of Moses, provided they followed what were called the Noahide Laws. James's decree was in this tradition. The Noahide Laws were a list of laws thought to have been given by God to Noah and his family. Since Noah predated Abraham, the Noahide Laws were thought to reflect God's will for all of humanity, as the entire human race descended from Noah. There were numerous slightly different lists of the Noahide Laws, but James's list of prohibitions loosely mirrors several of the items on the list of universal laws.[1]

Following the meeting, a letter was written to the Gentile believers announcing the results of the council: the Law of Moses and the requirement for circumcision were no longer binding upon Gentile believers. This was a dramatic event. The Law of Moses, the Torah, was the most authoritative part of the Hebrew Scriptures. Yet, led by the Spirit and based largely on the testimony of Peter, Paul, and Barnabas, the church accepted James's reasoning and set aside a major portion of the written Law.

Paul and Barnabas, along with two leaders from the church in Jerusalem, Silas and Judas, were commissioned by the Jerusalem Council to deliver its decision to the Gentiles in the churches in Antioch, Syria, and Cilicia. The decision brought peace to the situation in Antioch and confirmed Paul's authority to preach the good news to the Gentiles.

It's worth noting that Paul, in his letters, never directly mentions this decree from James, and though Paul insists on the prohibition against sexual immorality, he seems to interpret or apply the other commands from James a bit loosely, an indication that he may not have fully agreed with this decision.

It is interesting to consider this first theological debate in the early church. The debate was significant and resulted in a critically important decision made by the apostles and elders in Jerusalem. Those on one side insisted on conserving the tradition and laws of Judaism in this new movement, while those on the other side were willing to pursue a more "liberal" approach to the Gentiles as it related to circumcision and the Law.

Today many branches of Christianity still utilize councils or conferences to discern God's will and issue decrees based upon them; and some Christians lean toward conserving the traditions, while others are much more willing to reform and change those traditions. In Paul's time the decision of James and the council didn't fully satisfy either side. Those insisting on circumcision continued to insist upon it to challenge Paul. On the other side, Paul seems not to have insisted upon complete adherence to the decision of James and the council. This is not unlike the debates that denominations continue to have today and the response of those on either side!

Paul's Second Missionary Journey

Luke tells us that some time after delivering the decision to the church at Antioch, Paul said to Barnabas, "Come, let us return and visit the believers in every city where we proclaimed the word of the Lord and see how they are doing" (Acts 15:36). The Second Missionary Journey thus began with the need and desire to confirm the faith of the newly formed Christians in Galatia. But the journey would result in another conflict, this time between the two friends, as Luke goes on to describe:

> Barnabas wanted to take John Mark with them. Paul insisted that they shouldn't take him along, since he had deserted them in Pamphylia [on the first missionary journey] and hadn't continued with them in their work. Their argument became so intense that they went their separate ways. Barnabas took Mark and sailed to Cyprus. Paul chose Silas and left, entrusted by the brothers and sisters to the Lord's grace. He traveled through Syria and Cilicia, strengthening the churches. (15:37-40 CEB)

I'm grateful Luke includes this brief account. Barnabas and Paul had been close friends and traveling companions; Paul would not have been Paul were it not for Barnabas. Yet these two friends and Christian leaders had a falling-out. Barnabas showed grace to John Mark, his cousin, and perhaps hoped to mentor and encourage the young man as he had done with Paul. But Paul, in a very human reaction, was unwilling to forget that Mark had abandoned them on the first journey.

Often we put our leaders on pedestals, including our pastors, only to find as we spend more time with them that they are flawed. This has been true throughout church history. It is true of every leader I know today. In fact, sometimes serving in leadership can expose weaknesses or provide temptations, particularly pride. Paul's imperfections are a comfort to me, because they remind me that God uses imperfect people. His strengths, on the other hand, inspire me.

Though Paul and Barnabas went their own ways, Paul mentions Barnabas twice afterward in the epistles, and in his words there is no sign of bitterness. Mark, who was the reason for their split, seems ultimately to have become a trusted assistant in Paul's ministry.

I recall some years ago having a strong disagreement with a good friend who was also a pastor. I wasn't sure if we would be reconciled or not. It took a year of letting things cool down. It took each of us trying to understand why the other one felt and responded to the conflict as he did. It took an intentional decision by each of us to reach out to the other even when both of us thought we were in the right. And it took a willingness to forgive and to recognize that we both, in some way, had been in the wrong. Today I am grateful to count this man as my friend.

We don't know if Paul and Barnabas ever reconciled, but we do know that during Paul's second missionary journey he mentioned Barnabas to the church at Corinth in a positive way (see 1 Corinthians 9:6). Years later Paul would write to Timothy, "Get Mark and bring him with you, for he is useful in my ministry" (2 Timothy 4:11).* This passage points to some kind of reconciliation that must have occurred between Paul and Mark and likely between Paul and Barnabas as well. But Paul's second missionary journey would be taken without Barnabas, the son of encouragement, and instead Paul would be accompanied by Silas, the prophet and leader set apart by the apostles and elders in Jerusalem to convey their decision of the council.

The Book of Acts uses the name Silas, but Paul always refers to him by his Latin name, Silvanus. Paul describes Silvanus as his coauthor in 1 and 2 Thessalonians. In 2 Corinthians, Paul notes that Silvanus had preached with him in Corinth. And, as we'll find in a moment, Silas not only preached with Paul but was imprisoned with him as well.

I've suggested earlier that Paul wrote his Letter to the Galatians from Antioch in A.D. 49 or 50, in response to Jewish believers who retraced Paul's steps in Pisidian Antioch, Iconium, Lystra, and Derbe and sought to "correct" his theology by insisting the Gentile believers be circumcised. The theme of Galatians ties closely to the issues being addressed in Acts 15. Some scholars believe Galatians was written while Paul was on his second missionary journey, perhaps from Thessalonica or Corinth. We'll never know for sure. But it seems likely to me that Paul and Silas decided to revisit the churches in Galatia following the Jerusalem Council and the writing of Galatians in order to shore up the faith of the believers in the churches he had founded on the first journey.

Paul's Route

Take a look at the map at the beginning of this chapter to see where Paul went on the first phase of his second missionary journey. Paul left Syrian Antioch to travel by land, not by sea

* Many scholars believe that 2 Timothy was written after Paul's death by a follower of Paul. It may, however, include actual reflections from Paul or point in this passage to Paul's attitude towards Mark in the latter years of his life.

as on the first journey. Luke tells us, "Paul chose Silas and set out, the believers commending him to the grace of the Lord. He went through Syria and Cilicia, strengthening the churches" (Acts 15:40-41).

Paul headed north, visiting various churches he likely had preached in during his "silent years" of ministry. He continued on to his hometown of Tarsus in Cilicia, probably preaching and teaching with Silas there. If he had not stopped to preach and teach, it would have taken Paul a week to travel from Antioch to Tarsus. Stopping as he did, it may have been two or three weeks from the time he set out from Antioch to the time he reached Tarsus.

Tarsus city street

From Tarsus, Paul and his companion would have continued on the Roman highway through the Cilician Gates and across the Taurus Mountains all the way to Derbe. It was there that Paul and Silas met a young believer named Timothy. They invited Timothy to join them on their journey, perhaps in a role similar to the one John Mark was meant to play on the first missionary journey, both as an assistant and one to be mentored.*

* Acts notes that Paul proceeded to circumcise Timothy, whose mother was a Jewish believer and whose father was a Gentile nonbeliever. It is surprising, with all the concern in Acts and Galatians about circumcision not being a requirement, that Paul would circumcise Timothy. But some have pointed out that the circumcision would have made Timothy more acceptable in the synagogue, which would have been helpful on the occasions when Paul offered the good news there.

Paul would have crossed the Taurus Mountains on his route from Syrian Antioch to Derbe.

Paul, Silas, and Timothy continued their journey northwest across Asia Minor. Luke does not tell us of any preaching or ministry as they journeyed, nor does he give us their precise route, though we have clues. The distance from Pisidian Antioch to Troas, a city we'll read about shortly, would have been 350 to 400 miles, some of it through mountainous terrain.* Assuming that Paul and his companions walked fifteen miles a day, it would have taken them three or four weeks to make their way to Troas.†

Luke tells us they were forbidden by the Spirit to preach in two regions they might otherwise have gone into:

> They went through the region of Phrygia and Galatia, having been forbidden by the Holy Spirit to speak the word in

* A distance of 350 miles assumes a relatively straight route, but 400 miles allows for the roads to twist and turn through passes, along valleys, and by rivers. Mark Wilson's recent research suggests a distance of 550 miles.

† I'm assuming here that Paul and his friends walked 2.5 miles an hour for seven hours a day. This is a steady walk and allows for meals and stops.

> Asia. When they had come opposite Mysia, they attempted to go into Bithynia, but the Spirit of Jesus did not allow them; so, passing by Mysia, they went down to Troas. During the night Paul had a vision: there stood a man of Macedonia pleading with him and saying, "Come over to Macedonia and help us." When he had seen the vision, we immediately tried to cross over to Macedonia, being convinced that God had called us to proclaim the good news to them. (Acts 16:6-10)

This passage is of interest because it describes how God sometimes works in our lives. For some unknown reason the Spirit kept Paul, Silas, and Timothy from going into Asia. (Asia was the name of the westernmost province of Asia Minor). Paul was not to go to Mysia or Bithynia either. Just how the Spirit communicated this information is not revealed.

I wonder if there are times when you've been prevented from going where you wanted to go and doing what you set out to do, only to find that new and amazing opportunities opened for you as a result. Had Paul been allowed to enter Asia, Bithynia, and Mysia, he might have been kept from what became his fruitful mission work in the cities around the Aegean Sea.

Paul and his companions finally made their way to the port city of Troas. There at night, perhaps as Paul and his companions were sleeping, Paul had a vision of a man who was from the Roman province of Macedonia. The man called out to him, "Come over to Macedonia and help us" (Acts 16:9). Paul took this vision as a sign from God that the group was to leave Asia Minor behind and set out for a place where Paul probably had never been before, Macedonia.

Have you ever had a vision of your own Macedonian man? Several members of the church I serve had such a vision some years ago, only their Macedonian man was wearing a prison uniform at Leavenworth Penitentiary. They had a vision—a compelling idea that would not let them go—that our church was to be involved in ministry in the penitentiary and the adjacent Lansing Prison. Years later we now have dozens of people who are engaged in befriending, mentoring, and encouraging men at Leavenworth and Lansing every week.

A woman in the congregation recently sent me a note saying she felt compelled to serve persons who are suffering from mental illness. She had served in our congregation's ministry on mental health needs, and she felt moved that our church was to be doing something more. For this woman, her "Macedonian man" was women with mental illness.

Every day we are meant to be engaged in God's mission. Part of that engagement is paying attention and listening for God's voice through the voices of others who cry, "Come over here and help us!"

Paul, Silas, and Timothy Take On a Companion

The morning after Paul's vision of the Macedonian man, Paul, Silas, and Timothy boarded a ship from Troas and headed to the island of Samothrace, which was about fifty-five miles away. The next day they traveled another sixty miles and landed at the city of Neapolis, on the coast of the Roman province of Macedonia (which today is the northeastern coast of Greece).

An interesting thing happens to Luke's account of Paul's journeys, starting at Troas in Acts 16:10. See if you notice: "When he had seen the vision, we immediately tried to cross over to Macedonia, being convinced that God had called us to proclaim the good news to them." For the first time in either the Gospel of Luke or the Book of Acts, Luke speaks in the first-person plural, *we*. It appears here that Luke, the author of Acts, has just joined Paul and his colleagues.

Some scholars have suggested that Luke is simply quoting a source who wrote in the first person plural, but surely he had other sources from the life of Jesus or the stories of Peter who spoke or wrote in the first-person singular or plural, but Luke never uses "we" anywhere else in the Gospel that bears his name, nor earlier in Acts. The simplest solution to the multiple "we passages" in Acts, it seems to many, is that at this point Luke himself joined Paul.

William Ramsey, an archeologist and Oxford professor during the early twentieth century, suggested that Paul, Silas, and Timothy first met Luke in Troas but that Luke himself may have been from Philippi. Ramsey further suggested it may have been Luke whom Paul saw in his vision or dream that night in Troas. Why would Ramsey assume that Luke was from Philippi? It appears in Acts 16:40 that Luke remained in Philippi at the end of Paul's visit there. (Luke notes that "they" left Philippi, not "we.") He also notes that in Acts 20:6 the "we passages" pick back up in Philippi. Whether or not Ramsey's theory is correct, it's an interesting idea that Paul met Luke, whom he calls "the beloved physician" (Colossians 4:14), in Troas.

The "we passages" are found in Acts 16:10-17, 20:5-15, 21:1-18, and 27:1-28:16. (The events described, when Luke presumably was present, go beyond some of these passages, but the use of *we* is confined to these verses.) Interestingly, all the passages involve sea travel and mention small ports in the Aegean Sea, suggesting that Luke had a love of the sea and was a frequent seafarer.

At Philippi

Paul and his friends traveled from the port city of Neapolis to Philippi, about ten miles inland, which would have been an easy day's walk. The city's name came from Philip II, king of the Macedonian kingdom in the fourth century before Christ and father of Alexander the Great. In 42 B.C., just outside the walls of Philippi, Octavius and Mark Antony defeated Brutus and Cassius (who had killed Julius Caesar). Philippi was located along the Via Egnatia, the great Roman highway that spanned nearly seven hundred miles and connected the ancient city of Dyrrhachium (Durres in modern Albania) with Byzantium (today's Istanbul). The city was thought to have had ten to fifteen thousand residents, including many former Roman soldiers, but only a few of the city's residents were Jews.

Philippi was a Roman colony and an important city. Luke's account of Paul's visit to the city begins on the Sabbath, when Paul, Silas, Timothy, and presumably Luke went to the river to search for a Jewish place of prayer. Apparently the Jewish population was too small to support a synagogue. (Ten married Jewish men were required to constitute a synagogue). It appears that in places where there was no synagogue, Jews and God-fearing Gentiles gathered for prayer along the banks of the closest river or stream.

In Acts 16:13-15 we read,

> On the sabbath day we went outside the gate by the river, where we supposed there was a place of prayer; and we sat down and spoke to the women who had gathered there.

Surely there were at least a few Jewish men in Philippi, but it was the women who had come to pray at the river that day. Among those gathered, "a certain woman named Lydia, a worshiper of God, was listening to us; she was from the city of Thyatira and a dealer in purple cloth."

No husband is mentioned in the account of Lydia and her family being baptized. It appears that she was either a widow or divorced. I think of her as divorced, raising children as a single working mother.

Lydia's profession was selling purple cloth. There were several sources of purple dye in that period, but the cloth that Lydia sold was likely made from the secretions of a sea snail. It took thousands of these snails to produce a small amount of dye; hence it, and any fabrics made of it, were very expensive.

Because of its cost, the color was associated with royalty and the very wealthy. Philippi's location along the Via Egnatia assured that Lydia had access to buying materials and selling her wares.

On that Sabbath, Lydia was at the river with a group of women and her children, when Paul, Silas, Timothy, and Luke arrived and began teaching about Jesus. Paul taught that Jesus was the long-awaited Messiah, that he offered forgiveness of sins and new life, and that he was the embodiment of God's love. Paul's message moved Lydia deeply, and she trusted in Christ.

Following Paul's example, we have a significant ministry with divorced persons at the Church of the Resurrection. Some are women who were made to feel worthless, rejected, or unloved in their marriage and divorce. When I think of them, I'm reminded of my own mother and her life after divorce, and I remember Jesus' ministry with the Samaritan woman at Jacob's Well, near biblical Sychar. The Samaritan woman had been divorced five times, yet Jesus offered her "living water" and called her to be the first missionary to the Samaritan people.

Luke notes of Lydia's response when Paul preached, "The Lord opened her heart to listen eagerly to what was said by Paul. When she and her household were baptized, she urged us, saying, 'If you have judged me to be faithful to the Lord, come and stay at my home' " (Acts 16:15). Lydia became the first convert on European soil.

Baptism

There are three instances in Acts of entire families (households) being baptized after the head of the family put his or her trust in Christ: Cornelius in Acts 10, Lydia in this story, and the jailer at Philippi, whom we'll come to in a moment. Those who reject the baptism of infants and small children note that the word *oikos* in Greek, the word used by Luke for home or household or family, does not necessarily imply that there were small children present. They hold that baptism is only for those old enough to have a personal faith and to repent prior to baptism and that infants instead should be "dedicated" to God. And indeed it is true that we cannot know how old the family members were in the Acts households.

Those who affirm infant baptism note that *oikos*, as used in Greek, often includes children. Those who practice infant baptism see it as a sign that, for Christians, replaced circumcision. (In fact, Paul links circumcision with baptism in Colossians 2:11-12.) And just as circumcision practiced upon infants was as a sign of God's covenant with the child and their incorporation into the children of Israel, so too was baptism a sign of God's covenant and incorporation into the church.

We find no example of children being "dedicated" to God in the Book of Acts, but there are three examples of entire households being baptized in response to the parents' faith. For those who practice the baptism of infants and small children, parents are asked to nurture their children in the faith, and the church community pledges to do the same, so that day by day the child is growing in the knowledge of and faith in Jesus Christ. At an age roughly equivalent to the Jewish Bar Mitzvah and Bat Mitzvah, Christian children in traditions that baptize infants will receive special training and mentoring and then will be asked publicly to profess their faith in Christ and accept for themselves the gift of God's salvation that their parents accepted on their behalf as small children.

Hippolytus, a Christian theologian writing in A.D. 215, notes, "Baptize first the children, and if they can speak for themselves let them do so. Otherwise, let their parents or other relatives speak for them."[2] Hippolytus is giving basic instruction in the process of baptism, not making the case for infant baptism or defending it. His instruction seems to indicate that the practice of baptizing infants and small children was generally accepted long before the time he wrote. From his time on, there was agreement among church leaders that children were to be baptized. Even during the Protestant Reformation, when it seemed that everything was being questioned and required to be proved by Scripture, neither Luther nor Calvin set aside infant baptism. Likewise John Wesley, in the eighteenth century, accepted the practice.

In many ways, the two sides of the infant baptism debate focus on different understandings of baptism, and it strikes me that both can make a strong case for their practice. After spending several years exploring the issue biblically, theologically, and historically, I came to appreciate each tradition and don't believe this is an issue over which Christians should divide. I believe that both adult and infant baptism are means of conveying God's grace for us and the acceptance of that grace either by us or, with small children, on their behalf.

The Gangites River is about a third of a mile west of the ruins of ancient Philippi.* On the river, about a half-mile north of the archaeological site, is an Orthodox Church and baptismal site commemorating Lydia's baptism. In addition to a church and chapel, there is a beautiful outdoor area on the riverbank where groups can sit. If they want, individuals can receive or reaffirm baptism in the same river where Lydia and her family were baptized. The river itself is only a couple of feet deep at this location and maybe twenty yards across. A part of the stream is diverted to a smaller stream, where people can step into the cold

* In various commentaries and texts, the distances and even the names of the river and possible locations differ, and this has led to some confusion. The Gangites is sometimes also called the Krinides or the Krenides. Others have suggested that the Gangites is a different river 1.9 miles west of the ancient city's forum and that the river where the Orthodox church is located is the Krinides. I have been to Philippi twice and have studied the area around it on Google Earth, and I cannot find a second river 1.9 miles to the west that could have been the Gangites. There is a dry creek bed even closer to the city than the Gangites, just east of the theatre of Philippi. Foundations of a fourth-century church have been found there, leading some to believe that this might have been the location of Lydia's baptism. Finally, the reported distances vary dramatically in various commentaries from ancient Philippi to the river. The distances I've used were taken from Google Earth, using the closest point of the excavated city to the river and from the city to the location of the modern Orthodox church on the riverbanks.

and swift running water or lie back in the water. It is a powerful opportunity to connect with Lydia's story. (If you are using the DVD that is available with this book, you'll see me there remembering my own baptism.)

It's worth noting here that Paul and his companions treated the women at the river with dignity, offering Christ to them as they would have to any men gathered for prayer. Lydia, Paul's first convert on European soil, was a woman, possibly a divorced single mother. This woman went on to invite Paul, Silas, Timothy, and perhaps Luke, to stay in her home, which may have marked the beginning of the church at Philippi. Years later, when Paul would write his letter to the Philippians, he mentions two other women in the church at Philippi, Euodia and Syntyche, who apparently were in conflict. He describes these women as having "struggled beside me in the work of the gospel," and as his "co-workers, whose names are in the book of life" (Philippians 4:3).

I mention this because Paul is often remembered for statements about women keeping silent in the church and being submissive to their husbands. Some years ago my daughter, at the time just sixteen, said to me, "I hate Paul!" I asked, "Why on earth would you say that?" To which she replied, "He's a male chauvinist pig!" I reminded her that she was judging a man who lived two thousand years ago by twenty-first-century standards. The gospel that Paul was proclaiming led many women to understand that they were loved by God and had great worth. They were filled with the same Spirit that men were filled with, and as Paul himself wrote in Galatians 3:28, in Jesus "there is no longer male and female"

Yet Paul was still a man of his time, whose convictions and interpretation of Scripture led him to limit the role of women and to encourage mutual submission of husbands and wives to one another, yet still saw men as the head of their households. Sadly, at times in our history some of Paul's words would be used to limit women's roles and justify their subordination.

The baptistry at the Gangites River near ancient Philippi, where Christians recall Paul's baptism of Lydia and her family

But in Philippi, as elsewhere, we see that women were tremendously important in Paul's ministry and in the churches he founded.

The fact that Paul and his companions accepted Lydia's offer of hospitality, staying at the home of a Gentile woman who may have been a divorced single mother might have been seen as scandalous to Paul's fellow Jews and some of the Gentiles in town. But his actions signified a dignity, acceptance, and affirmation that Paul expressed to Lydia, just as her act of hospitality expressed her generosity, kindness, and earnest faith.

Unclean Spirits

Paul, Silas, Timothy, and Luke stayed in Philippi for "some days," ministering and teaching in the town and returning to the place of prayer at the river. Soon they met a "slave-girl," who seems to have been the first-century equivalent of a psychic or fortune-teller. People would pay her to tell their fortunes or prepare them for the future, and that money was a source of revenue for her masters.

As she met Paul and his companions, she began to shout, "These people are servants of the Most High God! They are proclaiming a way of salvation to you!" (Acts 16:17 CEB). It appears that at first the apostles accepted her witness as a positive affirmation. But she continued shouting after them "for many days." I love how the CEB notes, "This annoyed Paul." Finally, Paul turned to the girl and said to the unclean spirit in her, "In the name of Jesus Christ, I command you to leave her!" (16:18 CEB).

This is a perplexing story. Why did an "unclean spirit" prompt the slave-girl to cry out affirming words about the apostles? Why did Paul tolerate the unclean spirit and cast it out only after becoming annoyed?

In the accounts of people with unclean spirits in the Gospels when they come in contact with Jesus, they cannot help but announce who Jesus is, and they tremble in fear. Here the slave-girl, or the spirit within her, at first seems unable to resist declaring the truth about the apostles and whom they serve. Within a short time, though, her shouting becomes a distraction and even created a hindrance to the disciples' work. Paul invokes the name and power of Jesus Christ, and the spirit leaves her.

Recently when my wife was out of town, I was awakened in the middle of the night by the sound of something hitting my bedroom window. As I lay in bed, awakened and seized by fear, I could not move. I tried to shake the deep sleep from my mind and to figure out if the sound had been a nightmare or if I really had heard something. Finally I went back to sleep, assuming it had been a dream. Shortly afterward, I felt what seemed to be one of our cats jump onto the bed, but I knew that both cats were outside. Once more I was unnerved. You will either appreciate this or think I lost my mind, because I sat up and shouted, "If there is something here in this room, in the name of Jesus Christ, leave me alone!" I lay back down, and there were no more disturbances.

Was this a demon plaguing me or a reaction to some pizza I ate before bed? I don't know. I do know that on a couple of occasions I've ministered with people who were experiencing what seemed to them to be evil spirits troubling them. The descriptions they gave were much clearer and more explicit than my own experience I just recounted. I'm cautious and naturally skeptical, but I also wanted to take their experiences seriously. I encouraged them to consult with their doctors and to consider seeing a counselor who might help discover some traumatic experience that could be eliciting their response. But I also encouraged them to read Scripture and pray before going to bed at night, reciting words that would remind them of Christ's power over demons and God's power over evil. Then, if they had the experience again, I encouraged them to say aloud, "In the name of Jesus Christ, leave me alone!" I anointed them with oil, making the sign of the cross on their foreheads, and I prayed for God's protection and care for them. Finally I said, "If there is an unclean spirit plaguing this child of God, in the name of Jesus Christ, leave this one alone!"

In each of the cases, which had gone on for months, the individuals reported that the trouble stopped entirely within the first day or two of our praying together and of their practicing what we had spoken of. To my knowledge neither has experienced this since.

Punishment, Jail, and Hymns of Praise

As for the slave-girl in Acts 16, she was released from the unclean spirit, but it left her unable to make money for her owners, who clearly did not appreciate what Paul had done. It's interesting that in the Bible and in our own times, an encounter with the saving power of Christ often comes at an economic cost. We may find that our jobs, or the way we've performed them, are no longer consistent with the Christ we have come to follow. Or we may feel that certain ways of making

These are believed to be the ruins of the court where the magistrates met in Philippi and where Paul and Silas may have been tried.

or spending money no longer seem acceptable. (We'll see the economic impact of the gospel on Paul's own life once again in Chapter 5.)

In the case of the slave-girl's owners, they seized Paul and Silas and dragged them before the city officials, in a courthouse that has been identified among the ruins at Philippi as the likely place the apostles were taken. As Paul and Silas were taken there, a crowd gathered and attacked them. The magistrates, seeing the crowd, commanded that Paul and Silas be stripped of their clothes and beaten with rods.

The magistrates saw Paul's actions as violating another man's property and disturbing the peace, and they ordered swift punishment. The rods used to beat the apostles probably were a bundle of elm or birch branches strapped together. These bundles, known as *fasces*, were used to beat prisoners. Slightly larger fasces were a sign of power. Sometimes the fasces had an axe blade protruding from one side, indicating the power to inflict capital punishment.

Paul and Silas were stripped naked and beaten with fasces of perhaps six small branches tied tightly together. Afterward they were thrown into jail for the night with their feet locked in stocks. The beating would have left them bruised and bloodied, possibly with a cracked rib or two. It's likely that Paul and Silas were then shackled so their feet could not move and forced to sit up all night in the prison cell.

What would you be thinking as you sat in the prison cell that night in pain? What would you be doing? I suspect many of us would be disappointed with God. We might even be angry. Paul and Silas had given themselves to proclaiming Christ, yet they were humiliated, beaten, and now imprisoned for the night. But listen to what Luke says Paul and Silas were doing: "About midnight Paul and Silas were praying and singing hymns to God, and the prisoners were listening to them" (Acts 16:25).

How could they sing hymns to God at a time like that? Many of us would be complaining, "Why me, Lord?" and perhaps doubting the very existence of God. But Paul and Silas knew that their beating was not God's doing. They also knew that God doesn't typically stop people from doing evil things and that our faith does not keep us from suffering. But our faith certainly changes how we face suffering.

That night, Paul and Silas sang hymns of praise to God. In this darkness, both literally and spiritually, they knew that God alone could sustain them. As we will see, sometimes it's our acts of faith in the midst of the darkest times that leave their greatest mark on others.

Recently when I was leading worship, I looked up to see a woman who was battling an inoperable form of brain cancer. She was my age. I'd seen her not long before at her home, where she had told me about the effects of the cancer and her hope that she might live to Christmas. It took my breath away when I saw her in worship, for clearly she was in terrible pain. I could tell how difficult it must have been for her to dress and walk into church. But there she was, sitting next to her husband and singing hymns of praise to God. As I watched her in worship, her faith moved me deeply. It's how I imagine the other prisoners must have reacted when Paul and Silas sang their own hymns of praise at midnight so long ago.

There is a modern road that divides the ruins at Philippi. Since our roads often follow the old roads, it's likely that this modern road is very near the ancient Via Egnatia. The part of the ruins called the upper city, twenty feet above Philippi's agora or public forum, is where you'll see what is purported to be the prison cell where Paul and Silas were kept on that night nearly two thousand years ago.

Archaeologists debate whether in fact this is the prison, but in spite of the debate, when I stood at the site overlooking the ruins of the city, I found myself connected to the story and could imagine the sounds of Paul and Silas, wounded and in pain and yet singing their songs of praise to God in the darkness there. No one remembers the name of the magistrate who ordered Paul and Silas beaten, but people still come to the site and remember the remarkable faith of these two men.

The traditional site of Paul and Silas's prison cell in Philippi, where they sang hymns after being beaten and imprisoned

Luke tells us the story of Paul and Silas's imprisonment to remind us how we are to face suffering. Twelve years later, Paul would write a letter to the little church at Philippi. He would write it from a Roman prison cell as he was awaiting news of whether he would be sentenced to death.* And yet, despite his circumstances, Philippians is called Paul's "epistle of joy." He wrote to these Christians,

> Rejoice in the Lord always!...The Lord is near. Do not worry about anything, but in everything by prayer and supplication with thanksgiving let your requests be made known to God. And the peace of God, which surpasses all understanding, will guard your hearts and your minds in Christ Jesus. (Philippians 4:4-7)

More than a dozen years after being beaten and imprisoned, Paul was still praising God from a prison cell as he wrote to the church at Philippi.

I have several old Methodist hymnals in my library, each from the 1800s. They are very small and contain only words printed in tiny type. Names are engraved on the front, as many nineteenth-century Methodists who could afford it had their own hymnals. Along with Bible reading, singing hymns was an important part of spiritual life for the early Methodists. When they were happy, they sang hymns to God. When they were sad, they sang hymns to God. When they were afraid, they sang hymns to God.

In a similar way, Paul and Silas turned to God as they sang in the darkness of their prison cell at Philippi, proving that the most powerful witness you give to your faith is what you do in times of adversity.

---

* Scholars debate whether Philippians was written from Rome or Ephesus or elsewhere. I tend to favor the idea that it was written from Rome.

The Philippian Jailer

As Paul and Silas sang, an earthquake occurred. (This area was prone to have earthquakes.) The shackles burst loose, the prison doors flew open, and suddenly the jailer came rushing in, afraid that his prisoners had escaped. Roman jailers were responsible for their prisoners, and if they escaped, the jailer could be tortured and killed, so Paul and Silas's jailer was prepared to take his own life. It was better, he must have reasoned, to die by his own hand than to be tortured. But Paul and Silas stopped him, promising the man that no one had escaped. The jailer was moved by the integrity of the apostles, who apparently played some part in keeping the other prisoners in place while not escaping themselves. Relieved that his life had been spared by their integrity, the jailer asked, "What must I do to be saved?" (Acts 16:30). Whether he understood the full import of his question is hard to say. It seems more likely that he recognized only that Paul and Silas had saved his life by their actions, and he was asking what they sought in return.

But what they sought was not personal gain. Their response was simple: "Believe on the Lord Jesus, and you will be saved, you and your household" (16:31). The Greek word for "salvation" and "saved" is very broad and encompassing; it means to be rescued or delivered. Some Christians act as though salvation is simply about being rescued from death and delivered to eternal life, and at times this in fact is the meaning. But most often in the New Testament, salvation means so much more.

Christ came to save us from sin, ignorance, self-centeredness, arrogance, lovelessness, hopelessness, fear, despair, alienation from God and others, and yes, ultimately from death. There are three tenses in which Paul speaks of our salvation in Christ. We have *been saved* by what Christ has done in the past, in the moment when we trusted in Christ. That past salvation includes, among other things, forgiveness of sins, reconciliation with God, and a new beginning. Paul also speaks of our *being saved* in the present, a continuing action in which God is saving us, changing us, and continually delivering us. Then Paul speaks of salvation in the future, that we *will be saved*; we will ultimately be delivered from death.

I know I have been saved in the past as I trusted in Christ and became his follower. I also am cognizant of his continuing work in the present to rescue me from myself and all my weaknesses, character defects, and sins. We often call that work sanctification. And I trust that on some future day I will be completely saved, rescued from sin and self, and delivered from death to life.

Paul and Silas didn't sit down in the jailer's home and say, "We'd like to give you our ten-week course on what it means to be a Christian, and then you can be saved." They didn't lecture him on soteriology, or doctrines of salvation. They didn't ask if he fully understood a particular theory of the atonement. What they did that night was speak "the word of the Lord" (16:32) to that man and his family. The "word of the Lord," seems to mean here either the message of Jesus or perhaps a message about Jesus. Some ancient sources say they spoke the "word of God" to the jailer and his family. Typically in the New Testament, that particular phrase does not refer to the Bible but to a message about or from God that might be rooted in the Scriptures. In any case, the primary response of Paul and Silas to the jailer's question was an invitation for the man and his entire family to believe in the Lord Jesus.

Let's look at the word *believe* used here, because it reflects an important dimension of Paul's theology. The Greek word, *pisteuson*, can mean cognitive and mental assent to the truth of a statement, or it can mean trusting in a particular truth or individual. In this case the man was asked to affirm that Jesus is in fact *Kyrion* or "Lord"—a term which, in this context, means king or ruler or highest authority. It's a word that can be used for God, for the emperor, for high-ranking officials, but in this passage Paul and Silas told the jailer that salvation and deliverance came from believing that Jesus was *ton Kyrion,* in which *ton* in Greek means "the." Jesus was not one authority, ruler, emperor, or king among many; the apostles were asking the man to believe that Jesus was *the Lord*.

The jailer and his family were then given a brief introduction to Jesus. Based on what we know from Paul's letters and preaching, he probably explained that there is but one God, the maker of heaven and earth. God sent Jesus, who walked on this earth, taught us the truth about ourselves and God, called humanity to follow him, worked miracles, and eventually was hung on a cross and crucified by the Romans and Jews; who on the cross bore the sins of the world and demonstrated God's mercy and love for humanity; who was buried but on the third day conquered death and was declared with power to be the son of God. This Jesus, not Caesar, is Lord. We can find salvation by trusting, with both our head and our heart, that he is Lord—a trust that moves us to action.

Notice what Luke tells us in Acts 16:33: "At the same hour of the night [the jailer] took them and washed their wounds; then he and his entire family were baptized without delay." It's curious to imagine how the jailer and his family were baptized, since it was shortly after midnight. Did Paul and Silas walk them to the Gangites River? This seems improbable to me. It's more likely, I think, that Paul and Silas took water that the jailer had used to wash their wounds and poured it over the heads of the jailer and then of his family members.

It is sometimes taught that baptism must be by immersion, and clearly immersion is a wonderful way of baptizing. The church I serve, for example, has an immersion baptistery outdoors where we can baptize adults through complete submersion under water. However, we also baptize by sprinkling. We believe it's not the quantity of water that matters but the significance attributed to that water in the act of baptism.

The *Didache*, a late first- or early second-century document, offers among other things some instructions regarding baptism. ("Living water" below refers to running spring water.)

> Baptize into the name of the Father, and of the Son, and of the Holy Spirit, in living water. But if you have no living water, baptize into other water; and if you cannot do so in cold water, do so in warm. But if you have neither, pour out water three times upon the head into the name of Father and Son and Holy Spirit. But before the baptism let the baptizer fast, and the baptized, and whoever else can; but you shall order the baptized to fast one or two days before.[3]

The point is not to persuade you about a particular form of baptism, but instead to note that quite possibly in Acts 16 there were Christians who baptized by pouring of water on the head in addition to the standard practice of baptism by immersion.

Luke tells us that immediately after his family's baptisms, the jailer "brought them up into the house and set food before them; and he and his entire household rejoiced that he had become a believer in God" (16:34). I love the idea that after the baptism, Paul and Silas were invited to break bread with the jailer's family in a sign of hospitality and friendship. The prisoners had befriended the jailer and his family; the jailer had befriended the prisoners. And the result of all this—the faith sharing, the trust in God, the baptism—was that the jailer was overjoyed.

Paul's Character

The next day, the magistrates commanded that Paul and Silas be released from prison, but Paul was not satisfied. He informed the jailer that he and apparently Silas as well were Roman citizens. It was illegal for a Roman citizen to be beaten without a formal trial. Paul demanded that the authorities come and personally escort them out of prison. Frightened, the authorities did just that, begging Paul and Silas to leave the city. They left, but not before returning to Lydia's house to encourage those who had become believers during their short ministry in Philippi.

We learn a lot about Paul's character in this passage. I can picture him remaining in the prison cell, waiting for the same magistrates who had sentenced them. I can see the magistrates pleading with Paul and Silas to leave and not report them to the Roman authorities. We might ask why Paul did not tell the magistrates earlier, before the beating, that he was a Roman citizen. Perhaps he tried and no one would listen. Or perhaps Paul knew that accepting the punishment might actually serve God's mission—that his willingness to suffer for his faith might be used by God to great effect in that town.

This is precisely what Paul would say years later in writing to the Philippians from his Roman prison cell:

> Brothers and sisters, I want you to know that the things that have happened to me have actually advanced the gospel. The whole Praetorian Guard and everyone else knows that I'm in prison for Christ. Most of the brothers and sisters have had more confidence through the Lord to speak the word boldly and bravely because of my jail time. (Philippians 1:12-14 CEB)

During the early days of Paul's second missionary journey, we've seen some of his flaws and humanity. But here in the Philippian prison cell we encounter his great strength. Paul was called and he responded with power and passion and a heart for Christ. As we leave Philippi with its dramatic stories, Paul's second missionary journey had only just begun.

4

CALLED TO LOVE

PAUL'S SECOND MISSIONARY JOURNEY (2)

If I speak in tongues of human beings and of angels but I don't have love, I'm a clanging gong or a clashing cymbal. . . .

Love is patient, love is kind, it isn't jealous, it doesn't brag, it isn't arrogant, it isn't rude, it doesn't seek its own advantage, it isn't irritable, it doesn't keep a record of complaints, it isn't happy with injustice, but it is happy with the truth. Love puts up with all things, trusts in all things, hopes for all things, endures all things. . . .

Now faith, hope, and love remain—these three things—and the greatest of these is love.

—1 Corinthians 13:1, 4-7, 13 CEB

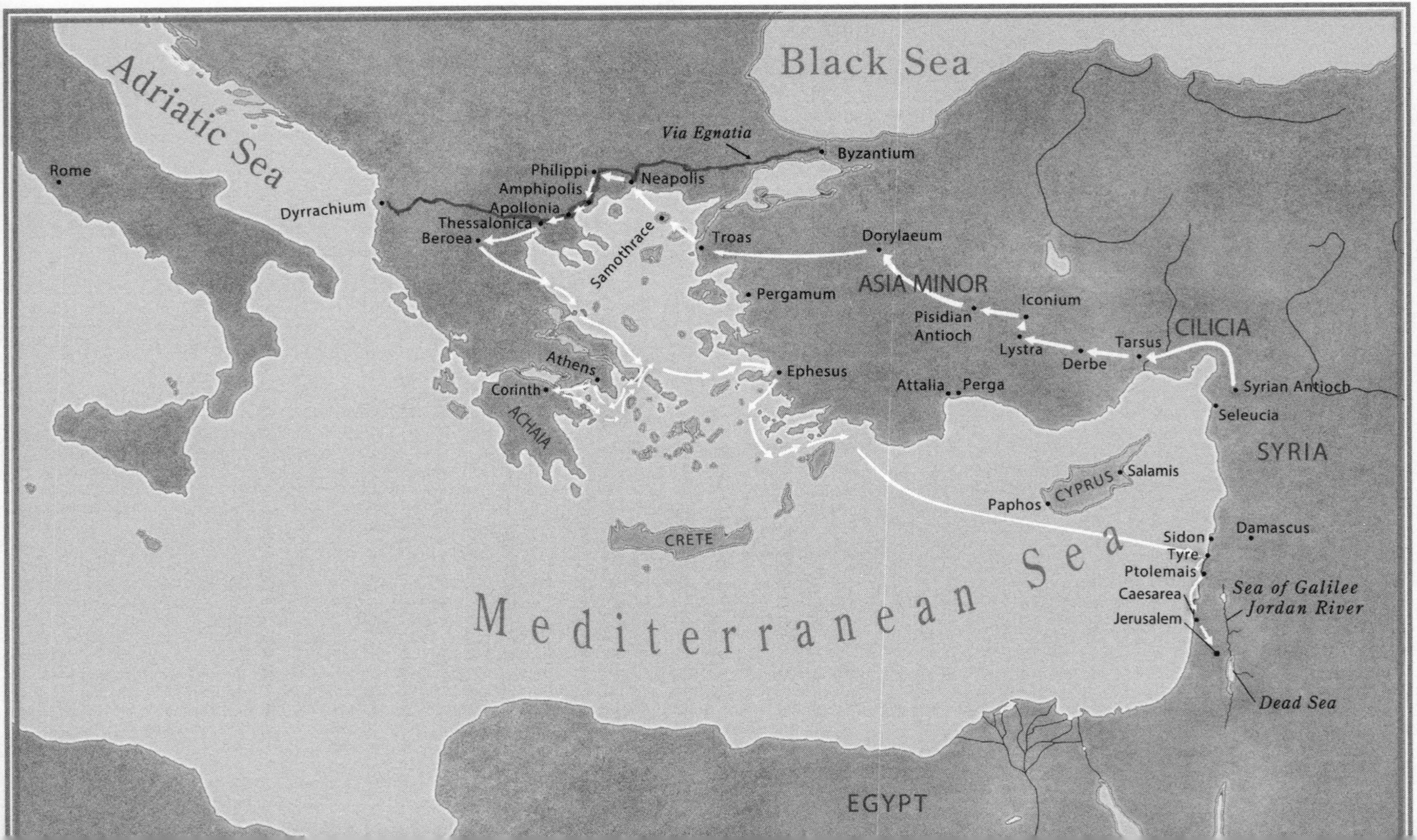

Black Sea
Adriatic Sea
Via Egnatia
Byzantium
Rome
Philippi
Neapolis
Amphipolis
Dyrrachium
Apollonia
Thessalonica
Beroea
Samothrace
Troas
Dorylaeum
ASIA MINOR
Pergamum
Iconium
Pisidian Antioch
CILICIA
Tarsus
Lystra
Derbe
Athens
Ephesus
Attalia
Perga
Syrian Antioch
Corinth
ACHAIA
Seleucia
SYRIA
Salamis
CYPRUS
Paphos
Damascus
Sidon
Tyre
CRETE
Ptolemais
Sea of Galilee
Caesarea
Jordan River
Jerusalem
Mediterranean Sea
Dead Sea
EGYPT

A.D. 67 Paul's Death

A.D. 52 Paul returns to Syrian Antioch

A.D. 50-51 To Galatia, Macedonia, Achaia

A.D. 50 Paul and Silas begin second missionary journey

A.D. 50 Jerusalem Council

A.D. 50 Conflicts over circumcision

A.D. 49-50 Paul writes Galatians?

A.D. 49-50 Paul and Barnabas return to Syrian Antioch

A.D. 49 Paul and Barnabas begin "first" missionary journey

A.D. 48 Paul and Barnabas to Jerusalem

A.D. 47 Barnabas to Syrian Antioch; with Paul at Tarsus

A.D. 38-48 Paul in Tarsus and region (est.)

A.D. 38 Paul meets Peter and James in Jerusalem

A.D. 35-38 Paul in Arabia, then Damascus

A.D. 35 Paul is converted on road to Damascus (est.)

A.D. 32 Paul arrests Jesus followers in Palestine (est.)

A.D. 16-22 Paul begins study in Jerusalem (est.)

5 B.C.-A.D. 10 Paul is born (est.)

5 B.C. - A.D. 10 Paul is Born (est.)

WE'VE HEARD THE WORDS at home, in church, and at countless weddings: "If I speak in tongues of human beings and of angels but I don't have love, I'm a clanging gong or a clashing cymbal. . . ."

These are Paul's words, and they're immortal. But what did he mean when he wrote them? What was he doing? Where had he been? We'll find out in this chapter, as Paul continues his second missionary journey—a journey that would take him to the historic cities of Thessalonica, Athens, and Corinth.

The Journey Continues

Paul, Silas, and Timothy left Philippi, and though they'd just been beaten and imprisoned, they didn't return to Syrian Antioch as many would have done. No, they traveled west on the Via Egnatia, the famous east–west Roman military highway.

There are still places where you can see the Via Egnatia, and guidebooks can direct you to places to hike major portions of it. The road was an ambitious project in the late second century before Christ, started by Gnaeus Egnatius, the Roman proconsul of Macedonia. As noted earlier, the road connected the Adriatic Sea to Byzantium. The Romans were master road builders, a fact attested to by the thousands of miles of Roman roads that can still be seen two thousand years after they were built. Today's highways often follow the ancient roadways, and the portion of the Egnatian Way that Paul traveled from Philippi to Thessalonica runs alongside today's highway E90 (also called A2). In fact, this highway is more commonly known as the Egnatia Odos (*odos* meaning way or road), a nod to the Via Egnatia.

Thessalonica and Beroea

Paul, Silas, and Timothy passed through the towns of Amphipolis and Apollonia on their way from Philippi to Thessalonica. (It appears they left Luke behind, as the use of *we* in Luke's account stops until Acts 20:5.) Traveling the ancient roads,

Amphipolis was about thirty-six miles from Philippi, Apollonia was another twenty-six miles, and Thessalonica another thirty-eight miles after that.* The three men likely carried tents, scrolls, clothing, and supplies on their backs, unless they were fortunate enough to have had a donkey to carry these things.

The routes they took were not flat but crossed hills and valleys. Taking into account the varying terrain, the supplies on their backs, and the stops they probably made, I suspect they would have walked about two days to get to Amphipolis, another two days to Apollonia, and another two days to Thessalonica. I don't know how you picture the Apostle Paul—I'd always imagined him a bit rotund—but I would suggest that during his missionary journeys, he was actually in pretty good shape. If Paul were wearing a fitness bracelet counting his steps, he would have ended each day with over 20,000 steps!

On arriving in Thessalonica, Paul and his friends found a synagogue:

> And Paul went in, as was his custom, and on three sabbath days argued with them from the scriptures, explaining and proving that it was necessary for the Messiah to suffer and to rise from the dead, and saying, "This is the Messiah, Jesus whom I am proclaiming to you." Some of them were persuaded and joined Paul and Silas, as did a great many of the devout Greeks and not a few of the leading women. (Acts 17:2-4)

Once again we find that when Paul arrived in a town he began to proclaim Christ in the synagogue, where there would have been a significant number of "God-worshipers," Gentiles who believed in and followed the God of Israel but who had not been circumcised. Once more we see that the people most drawn to Paul's proclamation of the gospel were these Greeks who worshiped God, as well as prominent women.

---

* These distances come from Mark Wilson's work, measuring the distance along the actual ancient roads that connect these cities. Google Earth provides slightly shorter distances.

It's likely that Paul arrived in Thessalonica with wounds still healing from the beating in Philippi, but once again he would quickly face persecution. Luke notes that "the Jews became jealous, and with the help of some ruffians in the marketplaces they formed a mob and set the city in an uproar" (17:5). Once more I would remind you that by "the Jews," Luke is speaking of some synagogue leaders, not all Jews. But clearly Paul and his message had a polarizing effect. He won over some of the Jews as well as many Greek God-worshipers, men and women, but his message and its appeal among the Gentiles led some of the Jews to strongly oppose him.

When the opposition turned violent, Paul and Silas may have been hidden by some of the new believers, including a man named Jason who appears to have been hosting Paul, Silas, and Timothy. With some of the synagogue's leaders in an uproar, Jason and a few others were dragged to the city authorities. The "ruffians" who had started the riot accused Paul, Silas, and Timothy of "turning the world upside down" (17:6). I love this description. In Paul's time and in ours, the gospel—the good news that Jesus, not Caesar or anyone else, is the Lord and that his kingdom is very different from earthly empires—should still turn our world upside down (or, in the words of a friend of mine, "rock our world"). How does the gospel do this today? In what ways does it challenge deeply held cultural values and norms?

I think about the riot that broke out in Bristol, England, the hub of the British slave trade in the eighteenth century, when John Wesley preached against slavery. Or the opposition faced by civil rights leaders in America in the twentieth century. I'm reminded of the opposition one church faced when the congregation sought to convert a house into a home for special needs adults, but the neighbors were afraid the home would lower their property values. Or the pastor who announced that gay and lesbian people would be welcomed in the congregation, then watched as some of his parishioners got up and left.

The new believers in Thessalonica feared for the lives of the apostles, and Luke tells us that in the middle of the night, the believers in Thessalonica helped Paul, Silas, and Timothy to escape. We can learn more about the apostles' time and ministry in Thessalonica by looking at First Thessalonians, the letter Paul wrote (with Silas/Silvanus and Timothy) to the new believers at Thessalonica. Keep in mind that the letter appears to have been written fewer than twelve months after their escape that night.*

> Our message of the gospel came to you not in word only, but also in power and in the Holy Spirit and with full conviction; just as you know what kind of persons we proved to be among you for your sake. And you became imitators of us and of the Lord, for in spite of persecution you received the word with joy inspired by the Holy Spirit.... As you know, we dealt with each one of you like a father with his children, urging and encouraging you and pleading that you lead a life worthy of God, who calls you into his own kingdom and glory. (1 Thessalonians 1:5-6; 2:11-12)

I encourage you to pause and read the entire first letter to the Thessalonians; it's a short letter that you can read in ten minutes. It sheds light on the ministry and message of Paul at this early stage of his work among the churches in Greece and Macedonia, and it shows his relationship with the early converts and churches, as well as some of the issues these new Christians were facing.

From Thessalonica, Paul, Silas, and Timothy traveled to Beroea, some thirty-six miles west by southwest of Thessalonica. This was a three- or four-day journey for the men. Upon arriving, they adopted Paul's usual strategy and preached on the Sabbath in the synagogue. Luke notes,

---

* Some give Galatians a later date than I have, which would make 1 Thessalonians the oldest book in our New Testament. For those who believe Galatians was written around A.D. 49 from Syrian Antioch, as I do, making it Paul's oldest existing letter, 1 Thessalonians is the second letter we have of Paul and the second oldest book of any kind in the New Testament.

> These Jews were more receptive than those in Thessalonica, for they welcomed the message very eagerly and examined the scriptures every day to see whether these things were so. Many of them therefore believed, including not a few Greek women and men of high standing.
>
> (Acts 17:11-12)

Today there are a number of Protestant churches and movements that call themselves Bereans or Beroeans, usually meaning by use of the term that they, like the Beroeans Paul preached to, seek not only to accept the good news of Jesus Christ but also to study the Scriptures diligently.

Athens

Within a few weeks or perhaps a month (we can't be sure of the time frame), some of the Jewish leaders from Thessalonica heard that Paul, Silas, and Timothy were preaching in Beroea, and they arrived to stir up problems for the apostles there. Paul left Silas and Timothy in Beroea, where they continued to teach and confirm the faith of the new believers. He was escorted by some of the Beroeans to Athens, about 210 miles to the south, a journey that probably took them two to three weeks.

It seems likely that Paul had never been to Athens, though plainly he was familiar with the great city. At that time Athens was not a big city (with a population of perhaps only twenty thousand, small compared to the much larger cities of Corinth and Ephesus), but it was still *Athens*. It stood for Greek culture and philosophy, and its history and importance were known throughout the world.

I can only imagine Paul's experience walking through this ancient and historic city for the first time. On the two occasions I've been there, I was awestruck to see its ancient buildings, many of which were hundreds of years old even by Paul's time—buildings that served as the pattern for temples and public squares across the Roman Empire. Paul would have walked past its Olympic stadium, site of the Panathenaic games held once every four years for nearly six hundred years by Paul's time.

It's worth pausing here to recognize that Paul's letters seem to show he enjoyed athletics. He routinely used metaphors from the games to describe or illustrate the Christian life. In his writings he draws upon metaphors from boxing, running, and wrestling, including training, competing, winning the race, and receiving the victor's crown. Surely he was excited to see the famous stadium of Athens as he entered the city.

As Paul entered the agora (public square) of Athens, he would have found temples, a synagogue, several sizable markets, civic buildings, and large open spaces in which people gathered for public discourse. On the edge of the agora was a rock outcropping dedicated to the god of war—Ares in Greek, Mars in Latin. The rock was called the Areopagus (Ares's Hill) or Mars Hill. The Areopagus in ancient Greece was both a ruling body—a court—and this rock hill below the Acropolis.

This rock outcropping is what is left of Mars Hill, where Paul was brought to testify before some of Athens's leading citizens.

The Acropolis, almost five hundred feet above sea level, towered over the city. Atop this large, flat, rocky area were the Parthenon and Erechtheion, the world-renowned buildings that continue to stand on this site. These were built more than 450 years before Paul arrived. Most of the temples atop the Acropolis were dedicated to Athena, the virgin warrior goddess, from whom Athens takes its name. The Erechtheion was dedicated to both Athena and Poseidon, the god of the sea. Also atop the Acropolis were two temples completed in Paul's time, which were dedicated to the goddess Roma and to Augustus. A thirty-foot-high statue of Athena stood atop the Acropolis as well. Nearby, beneath the Acropolis, was the massive temple to Zeus, the columns of which are still standing.

Luke tells us that as Paul surveyed dozens of temples and even more altars dedicated to various pagan gods, "he was deeply distressed to see that the city was full of idols" (Acts 17:16). These thoughts led Paul to the synagogue, likely the one whose foundation has been uncovered in the ancient agora of Athens. As noted previously, the agora was the public square in ancient Greek cities. It often housed the civic offices, temples, places for public debate, and marketplaces. When Luke tells us that Paul "argued in the synagogue with the Jews and the devout persons, and also in the marketplace every day with those who happened to be there" (17:17), he is speaking of the agora of Athens which was home to the synagogue, other public gathering spaces, and one of the marketplaces of Athens.

The synagogue was located just down the hill from a temple dedicated to Hephaestus, the god of craftsmen and metal workers. Though only the foundations of the synagogue still exist, Hephaestus's temple still stands above the synagogue. Paul argued with Jews and God-fearing gentiles in the synagogue, and then he went out into the public square, the agora, to offer Christ to the people of Athens.

Paul's Speech to the Athenians

Luke tells us that a group of philosophers began to argue with Paul. They took him to the Areopagus (Mars Hill), where some of their leaders asked Paul to explain his beliefs. Here we have a chance to see the rhetorical and oratorical skills Paul had learned as a young man in Tarsus. I find this to be one of Paul's most compelling speeches or sermons in Acts. It gives us a sense of Paul's approach and message when sharing Christ with those who worshiped the Greco-Roman deities. His words are found in Acts 17:22-31. (The text that follows is from the Common English Bible.)

> Paul stood up in the middle of the council on Mars Hill and said, "People of Athens, I see that you are very religious in every way. As I was walking through town and carefully observing your objects of worship, I even found an altar with this inscription: 'To an unknown God.' What you worship as unknown, I now proclaim to you. God, who made the world and everything in it, is Lord of heaven and earth. He doesn't live in temples made with human hands. Nor is God served by human hands, as though he needed something, since he is the one who gives life, breath, and everything else. From one person God created every human nation to live on the whole earth, having determined their appointed times and the boundaries of their lands. God made the nations so they would seek him, perhaps even reach out to him and find him. In fact, God isn't far away from any of us. In God we live, move, and exist. As some of your own poets said, 'We are his offspring.'
>
> "Therefore, as God's offspring, we have no need to imagine that the divine being is like a gold, silver, or stone image made by human skill and thought. God overlooks ignorance of these things in times past, but now directs everyone everywhere to change their hearts and lives. This is because God has set a day when he intends to judge the world justly by a man he has appointed. God has given proof of this to everyone by raising him from the dead."

The famous Acropolis of Athens, as seen from the top of Mars Hill

Paul began with an affirmation of the people: "I see that you are very religious." I take this as Paul's positive way of setting up the "case" for Christ, rather than criticizing Athenians for their pagan beliefs. I think this points to Paul's genius in sharing Christ. Too often Christians today feel compelled to criticize nonreligious people or those whose religion is different from their own. Paul did not do this.

Paul went on to find a point of connection between the Athenian's faith and his own. He noted that he had seen an altar "to an unknown God." Once again, Paul did not criticize this altar but saw in it an opportunity to connect the God he proclaimed to a god they already admitted might exist.

Paul then affirmed something central to Judaism and Christianity: God is the maker of all things and, as such, does not live in temples made by human hands. (Even Solomon, upon building God a temple, acknowledged as much.) The people at the Areopagus would have agreed with this assertion as well. Paul went on to note that the entire human race derives its existence from God, and that God "gives life, breath, and everything else" to us. Again, Paul's listeners would have nodded their heads in agreement. At this point what Paul said was consistent with similar conceptions of God held by other Greek philosophers.

Then Paul noted, "God made the nations so they would seek him, perhaps even reach out to him and find him. In fact, God isn't far away from any of us." In other words, the unknown or hidden God actually hopes to be found. This God came to reveal himself to us in Jesus and is quite near, as near as the air we breathe. I'm reminded that the Greek word for heaven signifies the sky—the area beyond the clouds—but also the air or atmosphere that is all around us. The pagan gods might live on Mount Olympus, but the God proclaimed by Paul was very near.

Paul then offered two quotations from the Greek poets, poets he no doubt had studied in his hometown of Tarsus: "In God we live, move, and exist" and "As some of your own poets said, 'We are his offspring.'" The first quotation may have come from the Greek poet Epimenides, who died in the sixth century B.C., and the second quotation from the Greek poet Aratus, who died in 240 B.C. Once more Paul was making the case for his faith by anchoring its truths in things the Athenian philosophers already believed. "We are his offspring" refers to the idea that all human beings are children of the one God, whether they acknowledge this or call upon his name. "In God we live, move, and exist" points, I believe, to the concept that we as human beings are dependent upon God, that God is the source of life and all that sustains it. To put it in modern terms, the sun that warms our planet, the oxygen we breathe, the very energy that holds everything together down to the smallest subatomic particles—all have as their source the power and will of God. In a moment, should God wish it, everything would cease to exist.

It reminds me of the quest in physics for a "theory of everything." The theory of everything, which I understand conceptually but when it comes to specifics is beyond me, would be a single theory hypothetically explaining all physical properties of the universe. No matter how much this elusive theory might explain, however, behind and beyond it is God. In God, Christians believe, everything lives and moves and exists.

Only after gaining such strong agreement on his case did Paul offer a brief and gentle critique of the Athenians' worship of deities made of gold, silver, and stone. Worshiping such gods in the past was a mistake they made that Paul said God would overlook. (This and much of the rest of Paul's speech demonstrates a God who is patient and merciful.) It's curious to note that the quotations from Aratus and Epimenides originally referred to Zeus. Paul, like other Jewish scholars before him, adapted Greek references that were originally written of Zeus, substituting the Hebrew and Greek words for God in their place. Paul was not saying that Zeus was the *same* as God, only, I believe, that when anyone spoke of the greatest or highest god, whether they knew it or not, they were referring to *the* God.

Finally Paul noted that with the coming of Christ, God sought to reveal himself to humanity. Therefore God is calling the human race to repent, or as the Common English Bible translates it, "to change their hearts and lives" (Acts 17:30). The Greek word for repentance is *metanoia*, which literally means "to think differently afterward," that is, to change one's mind after an encounter with Christ, resulting in a change of heart and behavior.

Some listeners sneered at Paul's words, but a few became believers, including a member of the Areopagus and a woman named Damaris. In Athens there is a street named in honor of Damaris. Tradition holds that she was martyred for her faith, and she is celebrated as a saint in the Orthodox Church.

Paul's ministry in Athens did not result in great numbers of converts. There are times when it is good to remember this. I regularly speak with pastors who are discouraged when they have poured themselves into ministry, sometimes for years, with what seems like very little to show for it. It's helpful at such times to recall that neither Jesus nor Paul was always "successful" in ministry, if by success we mean numbers. Numbers are not the only measure, nor always the best measure.

Phil Hollis was the pastor who led me to faith in Christ. For five years he pastored Faith Chapel Assembly of God Church in Overland Park, Kansas, a church of about 150 people. He spent his last thirty-two years serving a church of 150 to 200 people in Topeka, where he was loved by his flock. He never served a church of thousands of people. But he invested in and mentored a number young people who became pastors, including me. I was one of his Timothys. He helped me hear a call to full-time ministry. He even took me to visit colleges when my parents were unable to do so. In so many ways he laid the foundation of my faith.

Once, discouraged, he told me he had not had the impact he hoped to have on the world. I said to him, "Your ministry of calling, mentoring, and encouraging young people to follow Jesus was responsible for my faith, this church, and my ministry.... And I'm just one of a dozen young people you helped mentor and launch into full-time ministry."

Recently Phil was killed in a motorcycle accident at the age of sixty-three. I was honored to preach the message at his funeral and testify to what his congregation in Topeka and his family already knew—that Phil Hollis had a huge impact on the world, not by serving big churches but by serving small and midsized churches really well and by helping others hear God's call on their lives. That's why I dedicated this book to him.

Though few came to faith under Paul's leadership in Athens (and likely in many other cities where he preached as well), those who did come to faith would lay the foundation for a church that ultimately affected millions and millions of people. Athens would eventually become one of the important centers of Christianity, but it started with what Paul may have felt was a failed mission.

Corinth

From Athens, Paul traveled about fifty miles west by southwest to the much larger city of Corinth. While Athens had a population of perhaps 20,000 in Paul's day, Corinth's population may have approached 250,000.* Corinth was strategically located adjacent to the isthmus connecting the Greek mainland to the Peloponnese, a large peninsula to the south. The Isthmus of Corinth was approximately four miles wide, with the Gulf of Corinth on the Adriatic Sea to the west, and the Saronic Gulf on the Aegean Sea to the east.

Centuries before the time of Paul, a track had been built across the isthmus by which boats and their cargo could be hoisted out of the sea on one side of the isthmus and then ported across land on a kind of dolly pulled by slaves.† This track was called the Diolkos, and remnants of it can be seen to this day. It has been estimated that the process of porting a ship across the Diolkos might take as few as three hours or, perhaps more likely, as much as a half a day with as many as 180 men involved in the transport.[1]

If a ship were sailing from Rome to Athens, taking the Diolkos past Corinth would save 160 miles at sea, perhaps one to three days' journey by ship. More importantly, the journey across the Diolkos avoided significant risk associated with sea travel when ships passed around Cape Malea on the southeastern end of the Peloponnese. The weather and seas in that area were notorious for being difficult to navigate and it was considered to be "the most dangerous sailing zone in the Mediterranean."[2]

* Bruce W. Longenecker and Todd D. Still, *Thinking Through Paul: A Survey of His Life, Letters, and Theology*(Grand Rapids: Zondervan, 2014), 110. The estimates for Corinth's population in the first century range from sixty thousand to three hundred thousand in various sources.

† David Pettegrew, in his article "The Diolkos of Corinth," argues that the Diolkos was primarily used for transporting goods and not porting ships, but his seems the minority view. (American Journal of Archaeology 115 (2011) 549–74); http://www.academia.edu/7948794/The_Diolkos_of_Corinth.

The Corinth Canal was completed in 1893. In ancient times ships were pulled over land at this same location. The canal is four miles long and seventy feet wide at water level.

Even Homer acknowledges this when, in the *Odyssey*, he has Odysseus's ship blown off course at the cape: "As I turned the hook of Maleia, the sea and current and the North Wind beat me off course" (Book 9, lines 80–81). The Diolkos was replaced in the late 1800s with a canal that continues to serve ships passing between the Adriatic and Aegean.

The trade that passed through Corinth, along with occasional warships, brought great wealth and numerous settlers to the city. It seems likely that the sailors whose ships were being portaged at the Diolkos may have spent time and money in Corinth as they waited. Certainly those making their living from the transport of goods between the east and the west found in Corinth a place where they could flourish.

Strabo, the Greek philosopher and geographer who wrote several decades before Paul first visited Corinth, noted,

> Corinth is called wealthy because of its commerce, since it is situated on the Isthmus and is master of two harbors, of which the one leads straight to Asia, and the other to Italy; and it makes easy the exchange of merchandise for both countries that are so far distant from each other.[3]

The city of Corinth was destroyed in 146 B.C., leaving only its famous temple to Apollo. The city sat largely in ruins for the next century. Much of the city was rebuilt during the time of Augustus and the decades leading up to and including Paul's visit. The Corinth that Paul walked through was beautiful.

If Paul was distressed by the number of temples to pagan gods in Athens, he would have found no encouragement in Corinth. There were dozens of temples to various deities in the heart of the town and along the route up to the city's acropolis. A large temple to Augustus was built in Corinth, the foundations of which can be seen today. There were numerous other temples, but there were two temples for which Corinth was best known—one dedicated to Apollo, which stood on its site for more than four hundred years before Paul arrived (portions of which are still standing today) and a second temple to Aphodite, the goddess of love, which stood 1,900 feet above the town at the top of Corinth's acropolis.

Paul left Silas and Timothy in Beroea, while he traveled first to Athens and then on to Corinth. He soon met two Jewish tentmakers, a husband and wife named Aquila and Priscilla. They recently had been expelled from Rome with the rest of the Jewish population under a decree from Emperor Claudius (this occurred in A.D. 49), so they had come to Corinth and set up shop. Tents were made of goat hides, hence Aquila and

Priscilla likely were not only tentmakers but leather workers. Paul, being both Jewish and a tentmaker was welcomed by the couple, given a place to stay, and provided with work to support himself. Luke doesn't tell us if Aquila and Priscilla were Christians prior to meeting Paul, but if they hadn't been, they soon became Christians with Paul's mentoring. On the Sabbath, Paul attended the synagogue each week and sought to persuade both Jews and God-fearing Greeks that Jesus was the Christ.

Preaching and Teaching

Eventually Silas and Timothy arrived in Corinth, freeing up Paul to devote himself full-time to preaching and teaching. Luke tells us that a number of Jewish leaders became followers of Jesus under Paul's ministry, while others rejected Paul and the gospel he preached. Soon it was clear that he would no longer be welcome in the synagogue, and Luke describes what happened next:

> When they opposed and reviled him, in protest he shook the dust from his clothes and said to them, "Your blood be on your own heads! I am innocent. From now on I will go to the Gentiles." Then he left the synagogue and went to the house of a man named Titius Justus, a worshiper of God; his house was next door to the synagogue. Crispus, the official of the synagogue, became a believer in the Lord, together with all his household; and many of the Corinthians who heard Paul became believers and were baptized. (Acts 18:6-8)

Paul formed what was, in essence, a new synagogue, one which existed for Jews and Gentiles who believed that Jesus was the Messiah. You can imagine how the leaders of the existing synagogue felt about Paul's new church. To make matters worse, he formed it right next door to the existing synagogue. Ultimately the leaders of the original synagogue brought Paul before the magistrate, accusing him of "persuading others to worship God unlawfully" (18:13 CEB). But Gallio, the provincial governor, threw out the case.

This reference to Gallio in Acts 18 allows us to date Paul's visit to Corinth. Gallio was the governor of Achaia (southern Greece) from A.D. 51 to 52. During this time the provincial headquarters of Achaia was in Corinth. Paul's eighteen months in Corinth would have overlapped with at least part of Gallio's time as governor.

Scholars believe there was a large population of slaves in Corinth during Paul's time. Estimates range from one-third of the population to over half. There was much "new wealth" in the city, but it also seems clear that many residents lived at the lower end of society. It appears from Paul's first letter to the Corinthians, written a year or two after he left the city, that most members of the church were from the lower rungs of society. Read Paul's words in 1 Corinthians 1:26-28.

> Look at your situation when you were called, brothers and sisters! By ordinary human standards not many were wise, not many were powerful, not many were from the upper class. But God chose what the world considers foolish to shame the wise. God chose what the world considers weak to shame the strong. And God chose what the world considers low-class and low-life—what is considered to be nothing—to reduce what is considered to be something to nothing.

Paul wrote these words in part because by the time he wrote this letter, some in the church at Corinth appear to have been struggling with spiritual pride. (See 1 Corinthians 4, where this is an underlying theme.) Such pride resulted in divisions that had sprung up in the church, and the divisions and Paul's attempt to address them are found throughout 1 Corinthians.

The archaeological ruins of Corinth during the Roman period are amazing. Many of the streets Paul must have walked during his eighteen-month stay are visible. The remains of the theatre, markets, the place of judgment, and various temples are

The ruins of Corinth with the acropolis of Corinth (the "Acrocorinth") rising up behind them

clearly displayed. A handful of columns from the fifth century B.C. Temple of Apollo are still standing. Walking these streets today, it is easy to imagine the events described in Acts 18 and the situation among the Christians to whom Paul wrote his letters to the Corinthians.

Paul on Sexual Immorality

After visiting the ruins of Corinth, visitors can drive partway up the 1,900-foot acropolis that rises above the ancient city and then hike the rest of the way up. This acropolis was then and is today known as Acrocorinth. At the top was a spring that filled a pool of water, and today the spring continues to fill that pool, which is found below ground in a cave-like structure at the top of the acropolis. Not far from the spring was the famous Temple of Aphrodite, the goddess of love. This temple was said by Strabo, the Greek philosopher and geographer, to be served by a thousand temple prostitutes. Presumably the prostitutes would come down to the city and receive an offering for their services, which would support the temple.

The ruins of Corinth, from the acropolis

Many believe Strabo misunderstood an older story in reporting this activity, and they point out that a thousand prostitutes could not have lived at the Temple of Aphrodite, the remains of which suggest a temple of about 1,500 square feet in size. Whether or not Strabo was correct, we know that brothels were common in larger cities in the Greco-Roman World, yet only in 1 Corinthians, among all his letters, does Paul devote verses to addressing prostitution. This fact might substantiate the idea that sacred prostitution was practiced in Corinth, or at the very least that prostitution was a more widespread practice and source of temptation for the believers in Corinth than elsewhere. It appears that Corinth was known in the Roman world for its loose morals, perhaps because of the many sailors and traders served by the community.

Paul devotes more verses to the subject of sexual immorality in 1 Corinthians than in any of his other letters. (Paul touches on the subject in nearly all his letters, but he devotes more verses to the subject in 1 Corinthians than in all his other epistles *combined.*) The sexual values of the first-century Jewish world were far stricter than those of the Greco-Roman world.

Jesus raised the expectations of what constituted holiness when he taught that if we even look with lust upon another, we have committed adultery in our heart. At the same time, he demonstrated great mercy to those who were prostitutes and adulterers. I love that about Jesus: he calls us to very high standards but demonstrates remarkable mercy when we fail to meet those standards. Paul attempts the same in his first letter to the Corinthians.

There are many parallels between first-century Corinth and twenty-first-century America. Prostitution and other expressions of sexual immorality were a part of everyday life in Corinth; it was hard to escape them. In America today, Internet pornography is ubiquitous and, for many, becomes the gateway to sexual practices that promise pleasure but ultimately bring pain. The Greek word for sexual immorality that Paul uses in this epistle and others is *porneo*, the source of our word pornography.

When reading Paul's words in 1 Corinthians concerning prostitution and sexual immorality, it's helpful to remember that he is writing to Christians whom Paul himself led to faith during his eighteen months of ministry at Corinth. The fact that Paul devotes so much ink to these topics tells us that for first-century disciples of Jesus, self-control and self-discipline regarding sexuality was a struggle.

Christians today struggle with these same things. A 2014 Barna study found that 63 percent of Christian men view pornography at least once a month. The study also found that use of pornography seems to be accelerating among younger adults, with monthly viewing of pornography among men aged 18–30 reported at 78 percent.* The lure of this activity is strong, and there are many good Christians who find themselves stuck and unable to resist the pull of what Paul refers to as "sexual immorality." Sexual immorality can enslave us. It promises

* These statistics are drawn from a study conducted by The Barna Group for an organization called Proven Men. The study may be found at http://www.provenmen.org/2014pornsurvey/pornography-use-and-addiction/.

Temple of Aphrodite on the Acrocorinth

pleasure, but its pleasure is fleeting, quickly giving way to shame and pain.

Paul's words are timeless and have much to say to us in this age of Internet pornography:

> The body...is not meant for sexual immorality but for the Lord, and the Lord for the body....Do you not know that your bodies are members of Christ himself? Shall I then take the members of Christ and unite them with a prostitute? Never! Do you not know that he who unites himself with a prostitute is one with her in body? For it is said, "The two will become one flesh." But whoever is united with the Lord is one with him in spirit. Flee from sexual immorality. All other sins a person commits are outside the body, but whoever sins sexually, sins against their own body. Do you not know that your bodies are temples of the Holy Spirit, who is in you, whom you have received from God? You are not your own; you were bought at a price. Therefore honor God with your bodies. (1 Corinthians 6:13b-20 NIV)

I really appreciate Paul's words on this subject. He openly spoke of the struggles men were having at Corinth with sexual immorality. These were pastoral subjects shared by a shepherd seeking to care for his flock. He intended that his letters be read in the church. Today Christians are often uncomfortable talking about sexuality in church, and because of this we are complicit in the struggles so many have with sexual self-control. If we're unwilling to talk about it, we offer little help for men (and an increasing number of women) who seek the spiritual strength to avoid becoming slaves to their desires. Paul goes on in 1 Corinthians 7 to talk about sexual intimacy in the context of marriage, and again he speaks plainly. In fact, portions of 1 Corinthians 5, 6, and 7 are devoted to various aspects of sexual ethics. How comfortable are you with your pastor addressing the congregation on Sunday about sexuality? If the church is unwilling to talk about sexuality, where do our children, teens, and adults learn about sexual ethics and values?

By the way, what we call 1 Corinthians was not Paul's first letter to the church he started in Corinth, even though we refer to it as though it were the first letter. In 1 Corinthians 5:9 (CEB) we read, "I wrote to you in my earlier letter not to associate with sexually immoral people." So the letter we call 1 Corinthians was not the first time Paul had written to the Corinthians on the subject of sexual immorality.

Life in the Early Church

Reading 1 Corinthians and, to a lesser degree, 2 Corinthians helps us understand life in the early church better than perhaps any of Paul's other letters. Paul wrote 1 Corinthians from Ephesus while on his third missionary journey some two to three years after leaving Corinth at the end of his second missionary journey. (We'll explore the third journey in the next chapter.) The topics that Paul addresses in his Corinthian letters demonstrate his pastoral concern for the church and reveal the issues that the church—and Paul—was facing.

Paul starts by addressing divisions in the church that had developed since he had left. Factions had arisen within the two or three years since he left Corinth, as they do so easily in churches today. Further, disagreements among believers had resulted in Christians filing lawsuits against their fellow Christians in the courts. An eloquent teacher and speaker named Apollos had come to Corinth after Paul had left, and some in the church had decided that they were followers of Apollos rather than of Paul.

Some in the church believed the Spirit's works and gifts in their lives made them more spiritually mature than others. Some of the rich seemed to act as though they were more important than their fellow believers who were poor. There were what today we would call "liberals" and "conservatives," who were divided over questions of sexual ethics, the permissibility of eating meat that had first been sacrificed to the pagan gods, and other issues.

It is clear from 1 Corinthians 7:1 that a list of questions had been sent to Paul, and that 1 Corinthians contains Paul's answers to those questions. Paul writes, "Now concerning the matters about which you wrote..." and then proceeds to address various questions. We can infer the questions and see Paul's answers each time he writes "Now concerning..."

The first question, it seems, was whether being a Christian required one to avoid sexual intimacy even with one's spouse. Paul's answer is frank and clear: sexual intimacy is no sin in the context of marriage. In 7:25 Paul writes, "Now concerning virgins..." This question apparently had been about marriage. In 8:1 Paul writes, "Now concerning food sacrificed to idols..." In 12:1 he writes, "Now concerning spiritual gifts..." In 16:1 he writes, "Now concerning the collection for the saints..." Finally, in 16:12 he writes, "Now concerning our brother Apollos..."

Among Paul's best known and loved words in all the New Testament are those in the thirteenth chapter of 1 Corinthians. To this divided community Paul writes a passage he likely never imagined being read at weddings. He was trying to teach believers, some of whom had become a bit full of themselves, about the defining quality of the Christian life and the true evidence of spiritual maturity.

> If I speak in tongues of human beings and of angels but I don't have love, I'm a clanging gong or a clashing cymbal. If I have the gift of prophecy and I know all the mysteries and everything else, and if I have such complete faith that I can move mountains but I don't have love, I'm nothing. If I give away everything that I have and hand over my own body to feel good about what I've done but I don't have love, I receive no benefit whatsoever.
>
> Love is patient, love is kind, it isn't jealous, it doesn't brag, it isn't arrogant, it isn't rude, it doesn't seek its own advantage, it isn't irritable, it doesn't keep a record of complaints, it isn't happy with injustice, but it is happy with the truth. Love puts up with all things, trusts in all things, hopes for all things, endures all things.
>
> Love never fails. . . . Now faith, hope, and love remain—these three things—and the greatest of these is love.
>
> (1 Corinthians 13:1-8, 13 CEB)

I was taught years ago that a great test of one's spiritual life is to insert your name in place of the word *love* in 1 Corinthians 13, starting with "Love is patient." If you do so, how accurate are these statements about you?

One last side note: in the four years after Paul left Corinth, it appears that he wrote four letters to the Corinthians: (1) the earlier letter he refers to in 1 Corinthians 5:9; (2) the letter we call 1 Corinthians; (3) a letter he refers to in 2 Corinthians 2:3-4 as one he wrote through tears and in 2 Corinthians 7:8 as one that brought the Corinthians pain, a letter that many believe is 2 Corinthians, chapters 10-13; and (4) the more conciliatory portions of 2 Corinthians, consisting of chapters 1–9. These four letters offer us a window into the challenges, concerns, and conflicts faced by the early church and show us how Paul addressed them. We see his personality and faith coming through in remarkable ways.

End of a Journey

Eighteen months after Paul arrived in Corinth, he departed to travel back to Syrian Antioch. He boarded a ship at the port of Cenchrae, near the Aegean side of the entrance to the Diolkos, and set sail with his tentmaker friends Priscilla and Aquila. Their ship was bound for Ephesus, a journey of about 250 miles and perhaps two to seven days, depending on wind conditions and how many ports they visited along the way.

Luke offers this very brief synopsis of Paul's visit to Ephesus and the conclusion of his second missionary journey.

> After they arrived in Ephesus, he left Priscilla and Aquila and entered the synagogue and interacted with the Jews. They asked him to stay longer, but he declined. As he said farewell to them, though, he added, "God willing, I will return." Then he sailed off from Ephesus. He arrived in Caesarea, went up to Jerusalem and greeted the church, and then went down to Antioch. (Acts 18:19-22 CEB)

Paul's second missionary journey had been long and difficult. He had met people where they lived and had emerged with his faith stronger than ever. At the end of the journey, he had touched down in Ephesus and promised to return.

Paul would keep that promise in his third missionary journey, returning to Ephesus and remaining there for twenty-seven months. His impact on that great city dominates Luke's account of Paul's third journey, when Paul would shepherd the church, summon the Holy Spirit, and confirm his credentials as history's greatest church planter.

5
Called to Give

Paul's Third Missionary Journey

After some time there he left and traveled from place to place in the region of Galatia and the district of Phrygia, strengthening all the disciples.... [then] Paul took a route through the interior [of Asia Minor] and came to Ephesus.

—Acts 18:23; 19:1 CEB

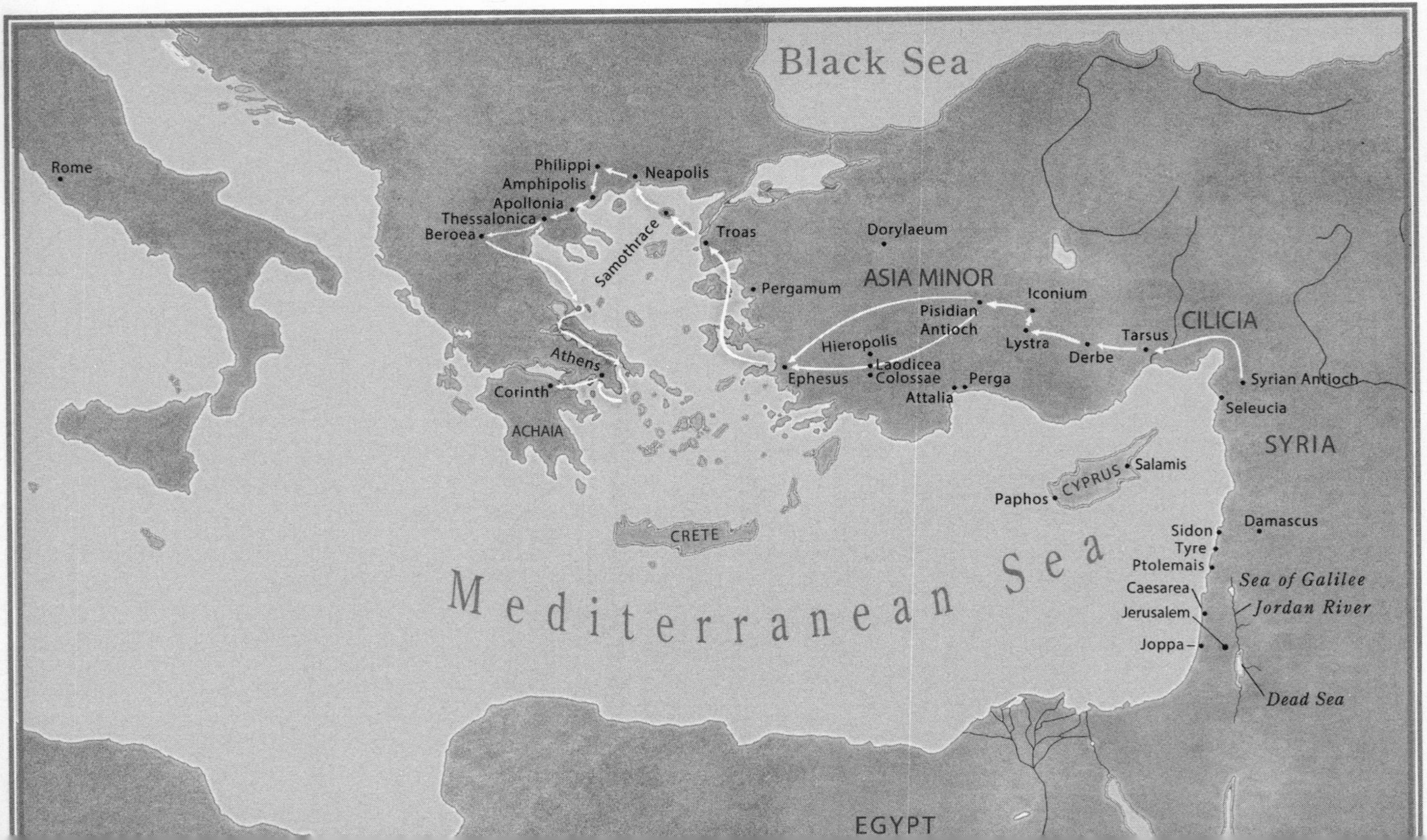

Black Sea
Rome
Philippi
Amphipolis
Apollonia
Thessalonica
Beroea
Neapolis
Samothrace
Troas
Dorylaeum
Pergamum
ASIA MINOR
Iconium
Pisidian Antioch
Hieropolis
Laodicea
Colossae
Ephesus
Attalia
Perga
Lystra
Derbe
Tarsus
CILICIA
Syrian Antioch
Seleucia
SYRIA
Athens
Corinth
ACHAIA
CRETE
CYPRUS
Salamis
Paphos
Damascus
Sidon
Tyre
Ptolemais
Caesarea
Jerusalem
Joppa
Sea of Galilee
Jordan River
Dead Sea
Mediterranean Sea
EGYPT

A.D. 67 Paul's Death

65

60

55

A.D. 53-57 Paul's third missionary journey

A.D. 52 Paul returns to Syrian Antioch

A.D. 50-51 To Galatia, Macedonia, Achaia

A.D. 50 Paul and Silas begin second missionary journey

50

A.D. 50 Jerusalem Council

A.D. 50 Conflicts over circumcision

A.D. 49-50 Paul writes Galatians?

A.D. 49-50 Paul and Barnabas return to Syrian Antioch

A.D. 49 Paul and Barnabas begin "first" missionary journey

A.D. 48 Paul and Barnabas to Jerusalem

A.D. 47 Barnabas to Syrian Antioch; with Paul at Tarsus

45

40

A.D. 38-48 Paul in Tarsus and region (est.)

A.D. 38 Paul meets Peter and James in Jerusalem

A.D. 35-38 Paul in Arabia, then Damascus

35

A.D. 35 Paul is converted on road to Damascus (est.)

A.D. 32 Paul arrests Jesus followers in Palestine (est.)

30

25

20

A.D. 16-22 Paul begins study in Jerusalem (est.)

15

5 B.C.-A.D. 10 Paul is born (est.)

5 B.C. - A.D. 10 Paul is Born (est.)

WHAT IS THE ECONOMIC IMPACT of large numbers of people coming to faith in, and seriously serving, Christ? How do an individual's values and spending habits change after becoming a Christian? Are there things Christians will spend less on, or perhaps even nothing on, after answering Christ's call? Are there things Christians will do more of with their money as their faith deepens? In this chapter, Paul is confronted by an angry mob as a result of the economic impact of the gospel at Ephesus.

Let's set out with Paul on his third missionary journey. On the journey he would visit and encourage churches he had founded on previous trips, but Luke's focus in reporting on the third journey is to tell us about Paul's time in Ephesus.

When we left Paul at the end of his second missionary journey, he had returned to his home church in Syrian Antioch. According to Scripture, he stayed there for "some time." Was it months or years? We can't be sure. At some point, though, Paul embarked by land on his third missionary journey.

We don't know much about the beginning of Paul's journey, which took him from Syrian Antioch through Pisidian Antioch to Ephesus and beyond. In fact, the first four hundred fifty miles are described by Luke in just one verse: "After spending some time there he departed and went from place to place through the region of Galatia and Phrygia, strengthening all the disciples" (Acts 18:23). So Paul traveled by land once again, passing through the Cilician Gates, across the Taurus Mountains, to the churches of Galatia that he had founded on his first missionary journey and had revisited on his second journey. These were the churches in the towns of Derbe, Lystra, Iconium, and Pisidian Antioch. This was now his fourth visit to these churches in just four years (except in Derbe, where it was his third visit during that same time).

From the Galatia region Paul continued on to Ephesus, one of the most important cities in the first-century world.* Of the ninety-seven verses in Acts that Luke devotes to the third journey, sixty-four are focused on Paul's time in Ephesus or with the Ephesian leaders. Paul also remained in Ephesus longer than he remained anywhere on his missionary journeys: either twenty-three months or three years. (Both time periods are mentioned by Luke.) Luke doesn't tell us who traveled with Paul on the journey to Ephesus, but we know from Paul's epistles who some of his companions were, at least for portions of the mission.

A Shepherd's Heart

Paul could have traveled from Syrian Antioch to Ephesus much more quickly and easily by ship. Instead he chose to travel by land. This entailed walking seven hundred thirty-six miles across mountains and valleys. The journey from Syrian Antioch to Ephesus would be like walking from modern-day New York City to Charlotte, North Carolina, or from San Francisco to Portland, Oregon. Why did Paul take this more arduous route? Why did he spend months walking on foot to Ephesus? Because it was the only way he could stop to encourage the believers in the churches he had started when he had been in Galatia. Paul didn't draw a salary from these churches. He wasn't being reimbursed for mileage! He did it because he had a shepherd's heart.

But there was one more thing Paul was doing in these church visits, something that became an important part of his third journey: he was giving instructions to the Galatian churches, the same instructions he would later give to the churches he launched on his second missionary journey, about taking up an offering to assist the believers in the Jerusalem church.

---

* By way of reminder, I've adopted the South Galatian Theory regarding Paul's travels, but I understand that a case can be made for a North Galatian Theory as well. It does not have a significant impact upon our study of Paul's story either way.

In 1 Corinthians 16:1-3, written months or even a year or two after Paul passed through Galatia, he wrote,

> Now concerning the collection for the saints: you should follow the directions I gave to the churches of Galatia. On the first day of every week, each of you is to put aside and save whatever extra you earn, so that collections need not be taken when I come. And when I arrive, I will send any whom you approve with letters to take your gift to Jerusalem.

As Paul had done at his Syrian Antioch church several years earlier, he was inviting the Gentile believers in the churches he was visiting on his third journey to receive a special offering to help the Jewish believers back at the mother church in Jerusalem. This offering likely was intended not only to meet the needs of the struggling Jewish Christian believers, but in so doing to build a bridge between the Jewish and Gentile believers. This offering was to become an important part of Paul's third missionary journey, a fact that we will touch on later in this chapter.

Assuming Paul spent a few days to a week at each of the churches he visited in Galatia, he would have arrived in Pisidian Antioch about two months after he set out from Syrian Antioch. From there Paul would have had two possible routes to Ephesus. Luke's description in Acts could be interpreted to mean either of these routes. Luke notes that Paul passed through "the upper regions" or "the inner regions"—both phrases are possible translations. The upper regions would indicate a northern route to Ephesus, while the inner regions could allow for a more direct and slightly southern route.

On the journey of our team from Syrian Antioch to Ephesus, we took the southern route that eventually passes through the Lycus River Valley. If this is the route Paul traveled, within a week to ten days he would have passed by the town of Colossae, just south of the Lycus River. There is no evidence that he stopped there, but my guide suggested that it would have been unlikely for Paul to have come this close to Colossae and not stopped, if only to eat or stay the night. The existence of the Epistle to the Colossians, if written by Paul and not a follower of Paul, suggests that Paul had not personally met any of the believers in the church there.*

As a side note, today Colossae remains an unexcavated tell, or archaeological mound. A well-worn path makes clear that many a visitor has hiked to the top. However, the ancient city did not originally stand on a hill; it was destroyed numerous times, and each time it was rebuilt atop the rubble. Over the centuries the city was rebuilt enough times that today it stands some one hundred feet above the ground level.

The unexcavated tell of the ancient city of Colossae, just a few miles from Laodicea

After its most recent destruction the city sat in ruins for centuries. Grasses claimed the dusty mound, and century after century of grasses left the tell of Colossae looking like an ordinary hill, though completely flat at the top. As we climbed up the path leading to the top of the tell, we spotted places where

* Many scholars believe that Colossians (and the lost epistle to the Laodiceans) was written after Paul's death by one of his followers. Others hold that it was in fact written by Paul while imprisoned in Rome (or possibly in Ephesus).

the soil had fallen away, exposing the buried remains of walls or buildings. Broken pottery shards littered the path. Standing on the hilltop, I longed for a spade so I could begin digging to discover the ancient city buried under my feet!

Several miles to the west of Colossae are the ruins of Laodicea. Had Paul traveled this route he would have seen and likely stopped in Laodicea, a much larger city than Colossae. The church there is one of the seven addressed in the Book of Revelation. While Colossae remains unexcavated, Laodicea is a magnificent archaeological site that continues to be excavated. While we walked its streets, teams of archaeologists were working to resurrect another section of the city.

Ruins of the ancient city of Laodicea

From Laodicea you can see the town of Hierapolis, which with Colossae and Laodicea was said to have been evangelized by Epaphras, whom Paul mentions in Colossians and Philemon.

Hierapolis is another magnificent site where locals still come to bathe in the warm springs, to attend concerts in the restored theatre, and to explore the ruins of the ancient city.

Regardless of which route Paul took from Pisidian Antioch to Ephesus, he finally arrived several months and six to seven hundred miles after he had set out on his third missionary journey.*

Visiting Ephesus

Estimates of the population of Ephesus during Paul's time vary widely. Some suggest it was the Roman Empire's fourth-largest city in the first century, following Rome, Alexandria, and Syrian Antioch (and just ahead of Corinth), with a population of more than 250,000 people. Others suggest the numbers were much smaller during Paul's time, perhaps 80,000 to 90,000, though some suggest much smaller still.† The city was four miles inland, and ships sailed up the Cayster River to a harbor off to one side of the river. Though the harbor has long since silted up, it can clearly and dramatically be seen using Google Earth.

The ruins of Ephesus are remarkable. Over two million tourists visit them each year, most of whom arrive by cruise ship in nearby Kusadasi on the Aegean coast. Buses bring these tourists from Kusadasi, and most enter Ephesus from the southeast, in the upper city near what would have been the state agora, a public square with government buildings; and adjacent to the Odeon, a performance hall for music, poetry, and other recitals. Nearby are the remains of the temple to the goddess Roma and to the Emperor Domition, who was likely emperor

* The shortest apparent distance across land from Syrian Antioch to Ephesus would have been around six hundred miles, but I'm guessing that the actual distance could have been 20 percent greater as the roads followed streams, rivers, and traversed mountains and valleys.

† It was my guide who suggested to me the numbers of eighty to ninety thousand. A wide variety of numbers has been published by various scholars. Seneca in the first century referred to it as the second largest city in the eastern part of the Empire (Scherrer, "Ephesus: History," 1026, citing Sen. Y. Ep. 17.2.21.)

when the Book of Revelation was written. Ephesus was one of the seven churches to whom Revelation was addressed.

Walking north and west, visitors move down Curetes Street just as Paul undoubtedly did many times in his nearly three years in Ephesus. Columns line the streets, with reconstructed temples and fountains on either side. Some of these temples and fountains also would have been there in Paul's day, while others were added later. Walking down Curetes Street gives modern-day visitors an amazing sense of the city as Paul would have seen it from A.D. 53 to 56.

Visitors taking this walk eventually come to the "terraced houses," ancient luxury "townhouses" in the heart of the city. Walking through the excavated homes, seeing the frescoes that adorned the walls and the mosaics that covered the floors, visitors get a sense of how the upper classes lived in ancient Ephesus. After passing these homes on the left and the ancient public

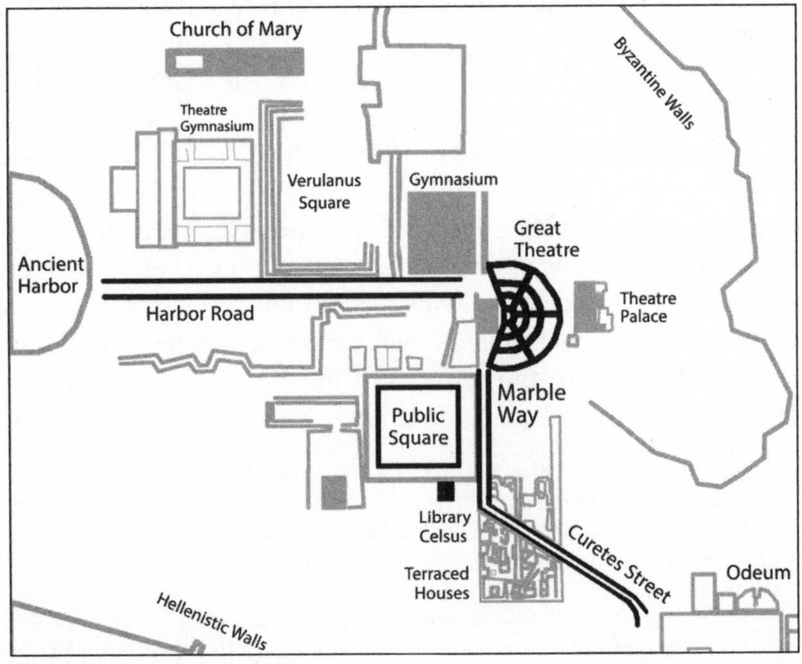

Diagram of ancient Ephesus

The façade of the Library of Celsus in Ephesus

toilets and brothel on the right, visitors arrive at the library of Celsus. This library, with its iconic façade and a collection that once numbered twelve thousand scrolls, was built after the time of Paul, in A.D. 135. Today the library of Celsus has become, with the Great Theatre of Ephesus, one of the best-known ancient buildings in the world.

The library stands at the corner of Curetes Street and Marble Street. Turning north on Marble Street, the ancient city square and shopping district are to the left. This square or public agora was not unlike many town squares in county seats across America, though it was considerably larger. Somewhere nearby, at a location not yet identified, was the "lecture hall of Tyrannus" that Paul rented for two years as a place to teach and minister to nonbelievers and believers alike. Continuing north, visitors come to the Harbor Road, a wide thoroughfare lined with columns that led, as its name indicates, to the harbor where the great ships came delivering their passengers and cargo.

Though the harbor has been filled with silt for centuries, if you walk to the end of the Harbor Road you can still find its

Curetes Street in ancient Ephesus

remains. Eventually you'll come to a marshy area, a reminder that great ships sailed in and out of this port a thousand years ago. Paul himself left Ephesus from this port after completing his stay in the city.*

At the intersection of Marble Street and the Harbor Road stands the Great Theatre of Ephesus. Those entering the city by ship would have seen the magnificent theatre straight ahead, astounding in its size and beauty. At its peak the Great Theatre seated twenty-five thousand people. It plays an important role in Acts 19.

Paul's Return

Paul had visited Ephesus at the end of his second missionary journey. At that time he had stopped at its port and visited the synagogue, leaving his fellow tentmakers and evangelists,

* In Acts 20:31 Luke records Paul saying he stayed in Ephesus nearly three years, but in Acts 19 it appears that Paul remained there for two years and three months.

Priscilla and Aquila, to establish a beachhead for the gospel. During the intervening time, Priscilla and Aquila had developed relationships in the synagogue and befriended an Alexandrian Jew named Apollos. We met Apollos briefly in the last chapter and will return to his story later in this chapter. While Paul had been gone, Priscilla and Aquila had been working quietly to prepare the ground for Paul's ministry.

Upon arriving in Ephesus during his third missionary journey, this time by land, Paul met twelve people whom Luke calls "disciples" but whose faith seems not to have been fully formed. Here's how Luke records the encounter.

> Paul…came to Ephesus, where he found some disciples. He asked them, "Did you receive the Holy Spirit when you came to believe?" They replied, "We've not even heard that there is a Holy Spirit." Then he said, "What baptism did you receive, then?" They answered, "John's baptism." Paul explained, "John baptized with a baptism by which people showed they were changing their hearts and lives. It was a baptism that told people about the one who was coming after him. This is the one in whom they were to believe. This one is Jesus." After they listened to Paul, they were baptized in the name of the Lord Jesus. When Paul placed his hands on them, the Holy Spirit came on them, and they began speaking in other languages and prophesying. Altogether, there were about twelve people. (Acts 19:2-7 CEB)

How fascinating. Paul met persons in Ephesus whom Luke refers to as "disciples," yet who had a very limited understanding of the Christian faith. The fact that they were called disciples seems to indicate that they had some knowledge of Jesus, but they had been baptized by John the Baptist (who had died twenty-five years earlier) or someone who had been influenced by John. It was a baptism of repentance, therefore, but not a baptism in the name of Jesus.

Paul explained more fully who Jesus was and what it meant to be a disciple. He also explained the person and work of the Holy Spirit, which seems to be Luke's focus in the story. Luke places a strong emphasis on the Holy Spirit in both his Gospel and Acts. It's worth pausing to reflect on this story and what it might mean for us today.

Many Christians today are disciples, but along with the twelve at Ephesus they might say, "We've not even heard that there is a Holy Spirit." Or perhaps they have heard of the Holy Spirit but know very little about it and have never invited the Spirit's influence and power to be at work in them. Looking over my library, I have a large selection of books on Jesus but only a handful on the Holy Spirit. When I was in seminary, we spent a great deal of time studying the life and teachings of Jesus, but very little time on the power and work of the Holy Spirit.

This lack of attention to the Holy Spirit may be one reason many of us, and many of our churches, have a faith that is a bit anemic. Acts begins with Jesus' promise to his disciples concerning the Spirit: "But you will receive power when the Holy Spirit has come upon you; and you will be my witnesses in Jerusalem, in all Judea and Samaria, and to the ends of the earth" (Acts 1:8).

This power that came from the Spirit was accompanied by sometimes dramatic experiences of the Spirit. In Acts 2, on the Jewish festival of Pentecost in Jerusalem, the Spirit came upon the followers of Jesus as they were praying in the upper room. It was as though a fire were spreading through the room, and strong wind gusting in their midst, and they began to speak in languages they had not known before. The believers streamed out into the streets and began proclaiming that Jesus was the Messiah.

This powerful experience of God's Spirit, deeply touching the believers, is attested to throughout the Book of Acts and Paul's letters. Paul mentions the Spirit more than a hundred times in his letters. In his Epistle to the Romans, written from

Ephesus during his third missionary journey, Paul writes, "For all who are led by the Spirit of God are the children of God" (Romans 8:14). In 1 Corinthians, also written from Ephesus, Paul devotes a great deal of time to describing the various ways the Spirit works in believers' lives, including prophetic words, the ability to heal, and speaking in unknown languages.

Paul teaches that the Holy Spirit dwells in each believer. Joy, peace, and power come by the Spirit. The evidence of the Spirit's work in our lives—what Paul calls the "fruit of the Spirit"—is described in Paul's earlier letter to the Galatians as "love, joy, peace, patience, kindness, generosity, faithfulness, gentleness, and self-control" (Galatians 5:22-23). If you do a search for the word *Spirit* in Paul's epistles you'll find an astounding array of verses describing Paul's experience and understanding of the Holy Spirit's work in our lives.

The Holy Spirit

As mentioned previously, I came to faith in Christ in a small Pentecostal church. The modern Pentecostal movement exploded on the scene in the early 1900s. The charismatic movement, a slightly toned-down version of Pentecostalism that emerged in Catholic and mainline Protestant churches, emerged in the 1960s. Both Pentecostalism and the charismatic movement were defined by their emphasis on the Spirit's work in the lives of individual believers and the Spirit's empowerment within the church. These churches also emphasized personal evangelism, Bible reading and memorization, heartfelt worship, the Second Coming of Christ, and a personal relationship with Jesus Christ. I suspect these expressions of the Christian faith arose because mainstream Christianity had so deemphasized the Spirit's work. I also believe that in these movements there were times when the Spirit's work, particularly ecstatic experiences, may have been overemphasized or at least overhyped. Faith healers laying their hands on believers who fell backward, "slain in the Spirit"; waves of "holy laughter" sweeping over congregations; an emphasis on experience without a corresponding emphasis on critical thinking—all these, I believe, were examples of excess or imbalance.

In spite of these excesses, I am profoundly grateful that in Faith Chapel, the small Assembly of God church I attended, I "heard that there is a Holy Spirit." I learned from my pastor and the congregation to invite the Spirit to guide and lead me. I learned that if I paid attention, I might actually hear the Spirit whisper to me. I came to understand that the Spirit empowers us, both personally and corporately as a church family. Thirty-seven years after I first attended Faith Chapel, and thirty-three years after joining The United Methodist Church, I continue to invite the Holy Spirit to lead, guide, and empower me each day.

When we baptize and confirm in The United Methodist Church, we lay our hands on the head of the one being baptized or confirmed. Often we anoint with oil (a sign, among other things, of the Spirit's presence and power) and ask the Holy Spirit to fill the one being baptized or confirmed. But I wonder how many, as adults, continue to invite the Holy Spirit to empower, work in, and fill them? In the time since your baptism or confirmation, have you intentionally sought the Spirit to work in your life?

I recently bought a new cell phone, because my old phone was running out of power by seven o'clock each night, if not before. Without power, my phone was nothing more than am expensive paperweight. This has always struck me as a good metaphor for the Christian life without the Spirit. If you are not "plugging yourself in" to avail yourself of the Spirit's power, your spiritual life may be running on empty. That "plugging in" happens as you invite the Spirit to be at work in you.

Every morning I invite the Holy Spirit to lead, fill, and empower me to effectively serve God for the day. Every week I walk through our sanctuary praying for God's Spirit to work through me and our worship team to help those who gather for worship over the weekend to know, love, and serve God. Luke wants readers of the Acts of the Apostles to understand that the Holy Spirit was critical in the spread of the gospel, and what was true in Paul's day is also true for us today.

Paul in Ephesus

Notice that after Paul baptized the disciples in Ephesus, he placed his hands on them and they received the Holy Spirit. This is the pattern that is seen throughout Acts: baptism, laying on of hands, and infilling of the Spirit. When I baptize people, regardless of their age, I immediately follow the baptism by anointing them with oil, dipping my finger in oil and then making the sign of the cross on their forehead. Following this, I lay my hand on their head and pray for the infilling of the Holy Spirit just as Paul did in Ephesus.

Terraced houses and floor mosaic in ancient Ephesus

After ministering with the twelve disciples in Ephesus, Paul made his way to the synagogue, as we have seen was nearly always his practice when he arrived in a new town. Luke notes that for the next three months, Paul "spoke out boldly, and argued persuasively about the kingdom of God," though some in the synagogue "stubbornly refused to believe and spoke evil of the Way" (Acts 19:8-9). It was then that Paul rented out Tryannus's lecture hall, teaching daily for two years.

Luke tells us very little about what Paul was doing, other than teaching, during his two to three years in Ephesus.* Tradition suggests that he may also have been imprisoned briefly during his time in Ephesus. (If you visit Ephesus, you'll be shown a hilltop outside of town that is purported to be the location of his prison.) We do know from reading 2 Corinthians that during his time in Ephesus, Paul made a trip to Corinth that is not recorded in Acts, a trip intended to address problems in the church there.

It appears that while Paul was in Ephesus, he was also mentoring others and then sending them to take the gospel across the province of Asia and beyond. Priscilla and Aquila were sent to Rome at some point during Paul's time in Ephesus. Epaphras appears to have been sent to his hometown of Colossae to start or lead the church and to start other churches in the Lycus valley, including churches in Laodicea and Hierapolis. Timothy and Titus, who were with Paul at various times in Ephesus, were sent by Paul to Corinth and elsewhere to strengthen new communities of faith. Paul was exercising, in the most expansive definition of the word, what would come to be called the office of bishop (in Greek, *episkopai*).

This picture of Paul and of the church at Ephesus, sending leaders out to start and lead churches and spread the gospel, suggests an approach that must be reclaimed in our "post-Christian" times. Churches and leaders must look at raising up new leaders, mentoring them, then sending them out to start new churches in underserved communities. One of the most effective examples of this I have seen was in Russia, where one independent Protestant church sent out dozens of leaders from its church to start new congregations in small towns surrounding its city.

Often in America this occurs when larger churches launch "satellite" locations in various communities. Church of the

* As noted previously, Paul was in Corinth for three months teaching in the synagogue, then two months in the Hall of Tyrannus, but in Acts 20:31 Paul notes he was in Ephesus for three years.

Resurrection, the congregation I serve, has three satellites as of the writing of this book, with a fourth launching in the next few years. We are one church in multiple locations. We share a common mission, vision, and values. The sermons come by video from our largest "campus." But each satellite location serves the community as if it were independent of the others. All are passionately committed to reaching nonreligious and nominally religious people. In many ways this was how Methodism spread in the eighteenth and nineteenth centuries: a congregation started, then from this congregation other new congregations were launched in nearby communities to form a "circuit" of churches. Has your church thought about sending members out to start a new congregation in a nearby community? Or has it considered creating satellite locations? A friend of mine serving a church of two hundred per weekend led his congregation to begin resourcing a much smaller congregation fifteen miles away, doing much the same thing we are doing with our satellite locations.

At Resurrection we have multiple smaller churches to whom we provide coaching and with whom we partner to share resources and ideas. Some of these smaller churches use our sermons on video, and others plan their own sermons. We also have a strategic goal of raising up a new generation of leaders. Our aim is to create in our congregation what some call a "culture of call," in which we invite people to consider a call to full-time Christian service. We believe that one of the keys to creating vibrant congregations is helping gifted young people consider God's call to full-time ministry. We plant the seeds for this in the third grade, when we give Bibles to our children. We emphasize God's call in our confirmation classes, describing the need for excellent pastors and full-time church leaders and helping our confirmands consider both the gifts needed for, and the blessings of serving in, full-time ministry. We have a program for teens that allows them to explore full-time ministry in the local church. We offer summer staff internships to college students.

We have set aside significant resources for seminary scholarships for those answering the call. And we mentor dozens of seminary students each year.

It appears that at Ephesus, Paul was identifying leaders, encouraging and training them, then sending them out to share the gospel and to start new churches and encourage existing churches. To do this, Paul taught in Tyrannus's "lecture hall"—the word for lecture hall in Greek is *schole*, from which come the words *scholar* and *school*. Thus we might say that during Paul's stay in Ephesus, he founded Christianity's first seminary!

The Healing and Exorcisms Ministry of Paul

In addition to Paul's work in Ephesus teaching, mentoring, preaching, and coordinating the Christian mission to the Gentiles, Luke tells us that "God did extraordinary miracles through Paul, so that when the handkerchiefs or aprons that had touched his skin were brought to the sick, their diseases left them, and the evil spirits came out of them." This mirrored Jesus' own ministry of exorcism and healing. Let's consider these first-century acts of healing and deliverance.

In the ancient world, medical and psychiatric disorders that defied diagnosis were often attributed to unclean spirits or demons. Our twenty-first-century image of these evil spirits comes from horror movies, and they conjure up terror. But in the first-century world where such spirits were thought routinely to be the causes of everything from fevers to infertility to epilepsy, it wasn't so much terror that these evil spirits conjured up in the hearts of people. Instead the evil spirits were seen as afflictions and viewed with frustration. The people hoped that by appealing to the gods, using just the right words or calling upon just the right name, they could force the evil spirit to flee, releasing the victim from its power.

First-century Jews believed they could exorcise demons by invoking God's name or the names of certain saints or even angels. As noted when we considered Paul's ministry in Philippi,

I don't deny the existence of unclean spirits, but it seems to me that often the causes of the various afflictions people experienced were not actual demons, but physiological, psychological, or spiritual maladies that were not diagnosed. Jesus healed people without feeling the need to explain that it was epilepsy rather than an evil spirit that afflicted a person. Either way, he delivered them.

If you read the accounts of Jesus' ministry, he often says to people he has just healed, "Your faith has made you well." Alternatively, in two cases Jesus forgives the sins of an individual who has been ill, and this makes the person whole. It would seem that at least some of the illnesses healed by Jesus, and later by Paul, were psychosomatic, psychological, or spiritual in nature. The healings started with the heart and mind of the individual, which led to an alleviation of the physical symptoms.

I've seen similar instances in ministry with people who struggle with anxiety disorders. Among the symptoms are those that mirror a heart attack or various pulmonary conditions. It is hard for the individual to breathe. The heart races. Palms get sweaty. Yet after running every conceivable test with inconclusive results, a physician suggests that anxiety may be the underlying issue. Patients often cannot accept the diagnosis at first; they know how real these symptoms are. And they're right. The symptoms are not all in their head. The brain is amazingly powerful, and it sends signals to various organs of the body. Often, when anxiety is the underlying problem, the solution may include medication and psychological treatment, but a person's faith and spiritual disciplines can also play a key role in healing.

In Ephesus during Paul's time, the city was known for the selling of incantations with secret sayings and instructions that were meant to unleash healing power upon those who needed assistance. These small spells or scrolls have been found in various places around the Mediterranean. An example from Egypt is a miniature scroll with this incantation: *"Give me your strength, Abras[ax], give me your strength, for*

I am Abrasax.' Say it 7 times while holding your two thumbs." Both the possessing of the scroll and the saying and doing of its commands were meant to bring deliverance to the speaker of the incantation.

There was money to be made selling these incantations. If you were hoping to become pregnant but had been unsuccessful, and you knew that in Ephesus you could purchase a saying that promised the likelihood of conception, how much would you pay for such a thing? If you needed your business to grow or your crops to flourish, or if you had some kind of physical pain, what would you pay for a magical incantation promised to deliver results? Ephesus seems to have been a center for trade in these incantations.

Into the midst of that place came Paul, preaching that it is Jesus Christ, not some demigod or incantation, who breaks the power of demons and heals us. Paul undoubtedly challenged the usefulness of the magic scrolls. Paul's ministry was having such a dramatic impact upon people in Ephesus, and so many were becoming followers of Christ, that it began to affect the sale and sales prices of these scrolls with their magic incantations. Here's what happened as a result:

> Many of those who believed now came and openly confessed what they had done. A number who had practiced sorcery brought their scrolls together and burned them publicly. When they calculated the value of the scrolls, the total came to fifty thousand drachmas. In this way the word of the Lord spread widely and grew in power.
>
> (Acts 19:18-20 NIV)

A drachma was a day's wages. If we calculate an average day's wages in the United States today at one hundred dollars, the value of the scrolls burned was *five million dollars!* What a statement about the impact of the gospel on these persons! The converts didn't simply sell their incantations or scrolls to someone else; they now believed that the incantations represented a false hope and power. Since they did not want to sell the incantations and thus deceive others, the converts destroyed them.

Some years ago a young woman who had devoted years of her life to practicing Wicca, a religion sometimes referred to as "white witchcraft" or modern paganism, began attending the Church of the Resurrection. Shortly after she decided to follow Jesus, she came to the church office to meet with one of our pastors. She had with her a large garbage bag filled with an assortment of things that represented her life in Wicca—books, incantations, ceremonial clothing, daggers, and more. She left these with one of our associate pastors as a way of leaving behind her previous way of life. She asked him to destroy these things. This is precisely what the people of Ephesus were doing when they burned their scrolls.

I wonder if there is anything from your previous life that you need to rid yourself of. Are there things that are a distraction or that aren't in keeping with your desire to follow Jesus Christ?

In some cases, our "scrolls" are those things we've previously trusted or made our source of security, but which we now have come to see can't really provide us with hope or help in the way that Christ does. These things might include lottery tickets, horoscopes, or psychic readings. Sometimes ordinary prescription painkillers can become addictive and long after they are no longer needed to control the pain, we find ourselves believing we can't live without them. For many of us, we've seen our monthly IRA statements as a source of security.

Several years ago I sat with a man who had worked hard, invested well, amassed a small fortune, and was now dying. His money had been the focus of his life and in a very real sense had been the source of his hope and security. He had worked hard to ensure that he would have enough money in retirement to travel, to maintain a certain quality of life, and to provide for his health and long-term care. But in his late fifties he was diagnosed with an illness from which he would not recover. He wanted guidance as he searched for a new source of hope and security.

Paul and Artemis

Many of the people in Ephesus, under Paul's ministry, found a new source of hope and help and security in their lives as they turned to Jesus Christ. This was true not only of those who trusted in spells and incantations but also of those who trusted in the pagan deities.

Ephesus was known throughout the Greco-Roman world as the city of the goddess Artemis. (Romans called her Diana.) Located about a mile outside of town was the Temple of Artemis, which was considered one of the seven wonders of the ancient world. Locals would often have statues of Artemis in their homes.

Artemis of Ephesus was the same as the Artemis worshiped in Rome, yet in ways she was distinctly different. The Roman Artemis was goddess of the hunt, while it is thought that Artemis of Ephesus was a fertility goddess, a mother goddess who blessed crops as well as marriages. The statues of her that have been found show a woman who appears to have, atop her head, the temple in Ephesus; and across her chest, a multitude of appendages that have been variously identified as breasts, bull testicles, or ostrich eggs (all symbols of fertility).

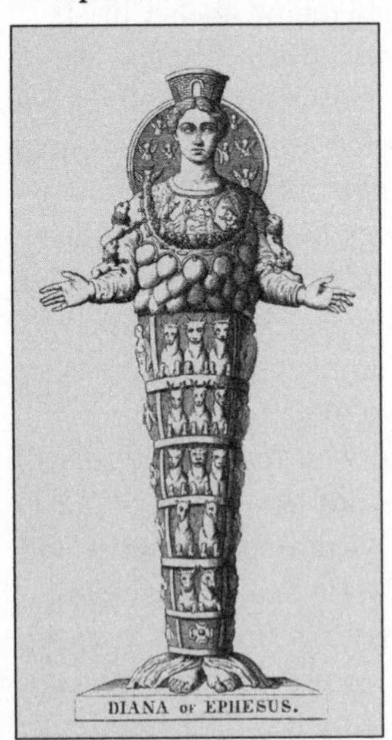

Figurine of the goddess Artemis (Diana) of Ephesus

People came to Ephesus from around the empire to honor Artemis at her magnificent temple. Ephesians were proud of their deity, and they reaped the financial rewards of religious tourism. Visitors coming to honor Artemis spent money on food, drink, lodging, and souvenirs.

After the burning of the magic scrolls, and following his exorcisms and healings, many began taking notice of Paul and the movement he led, known there and elsewhere as the Way. Among those who noticed were artisans who made the statues of the goddess. They began to fear the economic impact of people turning from Artemis to the Way. Listen to Luke, the master storyteller, describe what happened next.

> About that time there arose a great disturbance about the Way. A silversmith named Demetrius, who made silver shrines of Artemis, brought in a lot of business for the craftsmen there. He called them together, along with the workers in related trades, and said: "You know, my friends, that we receive a good income from this business. And you see and hear how this fellow Paul has convinced and led astray large numbers of people here in Ephesus and in practically the whole province of Asia. He says that gods made by human hands are no gods at all. There is danger not only that our trade will lose its good name, but also that the temple of the great goddess Artemis will be discredited; and the goddess herself, who is worshiped throughout the province of Asia and the world, will be robbed of her divine majesty." (Acts 19:23-27 NIV)

Which was more important to Demetrius—Artemis's honor or his own pocketbook? We can't know. What is clear is that, as with the owners of the slave-girl in Philippi, the gospel was having a negative economic impact on some people. Those affected economically sought to protect their economic interest, but typically they did so by arguing that Paul and his companions were offending the gods or promoting practices unacceptable to Romans.

The Gospel and the Economy

Is the gospel having any kind of economic impact in your community? For example, some years ago I preached a sermon on the connection between Christian discipleship and caring for the environment. I encouraged our members to set a goal of improving the fuel economy of their next car over their current car by 15 percent. This would lead to different choices in cars. Similarly, following various school shootings over the years, we've encouraged people to avoid violent video games or movies that promote violence. I also think about many successful businesspeople in the church I serve who choose to maintain a lifestyle many rungs below that of others earning the same income, so they can give more to God's work, to causes that promote justice, and to efforts to address poverty. At Christmas we invite our members to give an amount equal to what they spend on their family to projects that work to alleviate poverty—this typically means spending less at the shopping center. All these initiatives have an economic impact.

When I think about the potential economic impact of the gospel, I'm reminded of the 1950s and 1960s, when middle-class African Americans began purchasing homes in Kansas City neighborhoods. Fear gripped some of the existing homeowners, who worried that their home values would deteriorate. Many also feared racial integration itself and consequently put their homes on the market. An African American family would move in, and for sale signs would spring up. The result was a kind of self-fulfilling prophecy in which home prices did in fact plummet, not because the African American families moved in but because the white families were afraid. Faith could have made a difference in those neighborhoods, and it did in some. Of course, it would have taken a strong faith and commitment to integration to set aside the fear of seeing one's home price decline in order to remain in a changing neighborhood, yet many did just that.

In Ephesus, when the makers and sellers of magic scrolls and Artemis trinkets found their livelihoods threatened by the preaching of Paul, they rushed to the Great Theatre. Angered by the threat to their livelihood, they chose to characterize Paul's activities as disrespect to Artemis. They began shouting,

"Great is Artemis of the Ephesians!" (19:28). The city was thrown into an uproar.

Those of Paul's associates who could be found were seized and dragged to the theatre, where a huge crowd of townspeople gathered. Paul sought to go to address the crowd, but his friends would not permit him. Luke mentions, "Even some officials of the province of Asia, who were Paul's friends, sent word to him, begging him not to venture into the theater" (19:31 NIV). (It's interesting to note that some of the public officials had become friends of Paul, which points to the esteem many had for him.) Paul was restrained from going before the crowd, which for two hours continued to shout, "Great is Artemis of the Ephesians!"

The Great Theatre of Ephesus

Eventually the city manager arrived, spoke to the crowd, and warned them that it was an unlawful assembly. He informed the protesters that the followers of the Way were not guilty of robbing temples or insulting Artemis, and if there were any charges that needed to be brought, then Demetrius should do so in the courts, not in the streets. The crowd was sent home.

Paul writes in 2 Corinthians about his time in Ephesus (which he refers to as Asia, the province in which Ephesus was located): "We do not want you to be unaware, brothers and sisters, of the affliction we experienced in Asia; for we were so utterly, unbearably crushed that we despaired of life itself" (2 Corinthians 1:8). Later in the same letter he writes of his perspective on the hardships he faced, "We are afflicted in every way, but not crushed; perplexed, but not driven to despair; persecuted, but not forsaken; struck down, but not destroyed" (4:8-9).

Leaving Ephesus

Paul finally left Ephesus, traveling to Macedonia, visiting the churches he founded on his second journey starting with Troas in Asia Minor; continuing to Philippi, Amphipolis, Apollonia, Thessalonica, and Beroea; and then ultimately making his way to Corinth. The purpose of these visits was not merely pastoral. Paul had sent word a year earlier that he would be coming to receive a collection from each church to assist the Jewish believers at the mother church in Jerusalem. He had previously sent Titus and others with this message. We have an excellent record of Paul's approach to this offering in 2 Corinthians 8–9, chapters which are almost entirely devoted to Paul's teaching and request related to the offering. As you read these chapters you'll see there is an urgency to Paul's request concerning the collection for Jerusalem.

This offering was personal for Paul. It wasn't simply about providing aid for the Jerusalem church. It was also a way of building a bridge and demonstrating to the apostles the earnest faith and love of the Gentiles. I suspect the collection was about something deeper still. Some in the Jerusalem church continued to struggle with Paul's message, particularly as it related to circumcision and the Law. Some no doubt still saw him as the man who gave approval for Stephen's death and who subsequently persecuted the church in Jerusalem. I believe the urgency Paul felt about the collection sprang from his seeing it as an opportunity to bless the church he had once tried to destroy, while demonstrating the earnestness of his faith and the faith of the Gentile believers.

After receiving the collection from the Macedonian churches, Paul arrived in Corinth and remained at the church there for three months. By way of reminder, shortly after Paul left Corinth four or five years earlier, the church had begun experiencing conflicts and questions. Divisions had arisen when Apollos arrived from Ephesus and sought to lead and teach the church. There were challenges regarding sexual immorality in the church. Even greater divisions developed when some Jewish believers came claiming to be apostles and "correcting" Paul's theology, leading some in the church there to challenge Paul's authority and theology. It was personally painful to Paul that some in the church at Corinth were now questioning his motives, his teaching, and his apostleship. Paul's writings in First and Second Corinthians shine a light on the struggles of the early churches, but they also allow us to see Paul's humanity—his hurt and anger, his facetiousness and humility, his passion and pride.

By the time Paul arrived in Corinth after visiting the Macedonian churches, he had already exchanged more conciliatory correspondence with the Corinthians. Luke doesn't tell us, but we can suppose that Paul's three months at Corinth were a time of healing and reconciliation between the church and her founding apostle. Upon departing Corinth, Paul retraced his steps back through Macedonia, to Troas, and then to Miletus, a town near Ephesus, where Paul called for the church leaders at Ephesus to join him.

By this time Paul was determined to return to Jerusalem by Pentecost in late spring. He and his traveling associates were carrying with them the collection for the Jerusalem church. In addition, Paul had received several messages from the Spirit in several of the Macedonian churches that "prisons and troubles" awaited him in Jerusalem (Acts 20:23 CEB).

Luke records Paul's final words to the leaders of Ephesus, then tells us that Paul "knelt down with them all and prayed. There was much weeping among them all; they embraced Paul and kissed him, grieving especially because of what he had said, that they would not see him again. Then they brought him to the ship" (Acts 20:36-38).

In Acts 21, Luke describes the remainder of Paul's journey to Jerusalem, including more warnings from believers that he would face suffering there. Paul pressed on, finally reaching Jerusalem, where the brothers and sisters "welcomed us warmly" (21:17). In the next and final chapter, we'll see that the warm welcome did not last and that Paul's journey to Jerusalem would in fact lead to his death.

6
Called to Be Faithful

Paul's Death and Legacy

We and the local believers urged Paul not to go up to Jerusalem. Paul replied, "Why are you doing this? Why are you weeping and breaking my heart? I'm ready not only to be arrested but even to die in Jerusalem for the sake of the name of the Lord Jesus."

—Acts 21:12-13 CEB

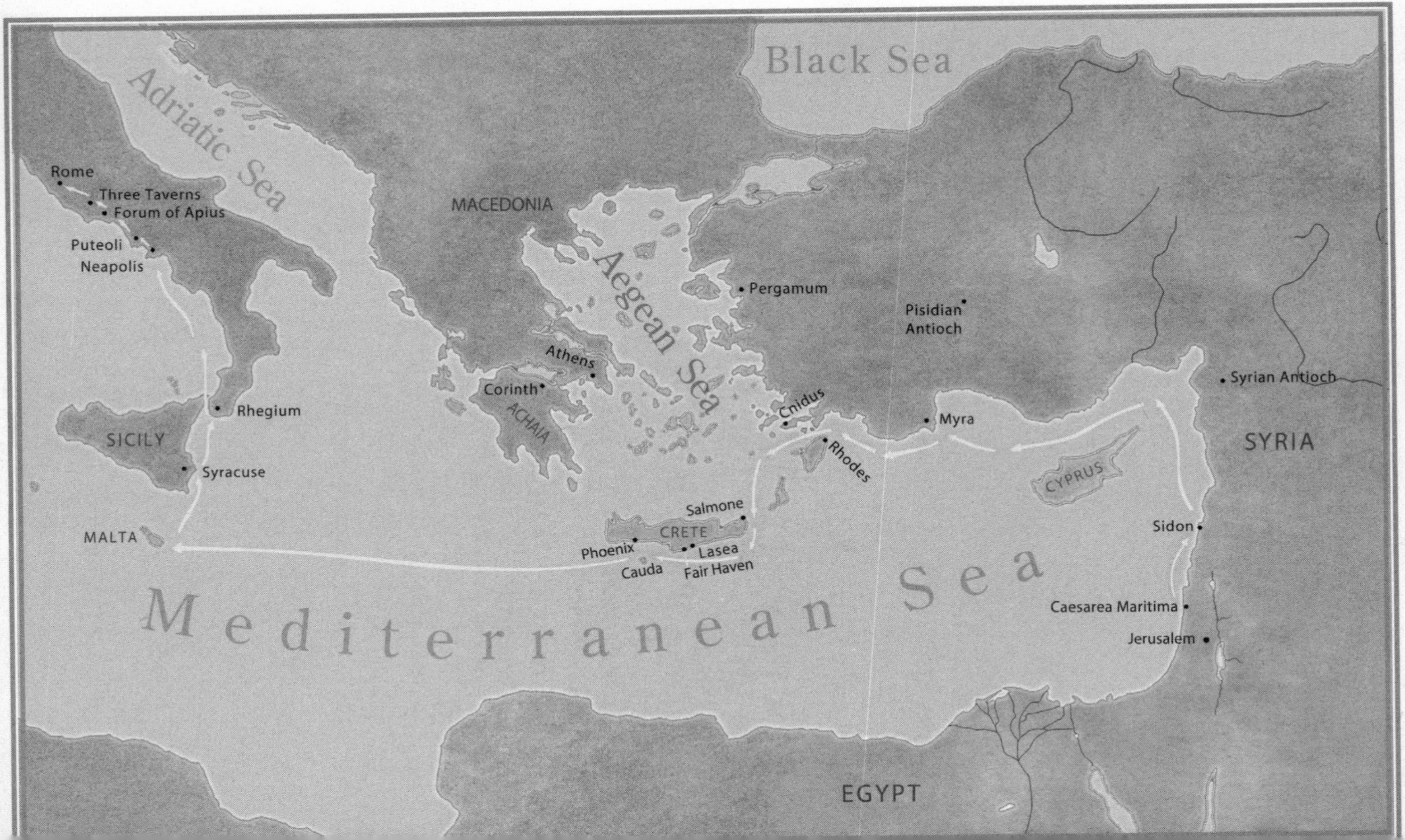

Black Sea
Adriatic Sea
Rome
Three Taverns
Forum of Apius
Puteoli
Neapolis
MACEDONIA
Aegean Sea
Pergamum
Pisidian Antioch
Syrian Antioch
Athens
Corinth
ACHAIA
Rhegium
SICILY
Syracuse
Cnidus
Myra
Rhodes
SYRIA
CYPRUS
Salmone
CRETE
Phoenix
Lasea
Cauda
Fair Haven
MALTA
Sidon
Mediterranean Sea
Caesarea Maritima
Jerusalem
EGYPT

A.D. 67 Paul's Death

A.D. 65 Paul's death

A.D. 62-65 Paul released? Visit to Spain?

A.D. 60-62 Paul under house arrest in Rome

A.D. 59-60 Paul's journey to Rome

A.D. 57-59 Paul imprisoned in Caesarea Maritima

A.D. 57 Paul arrested in Jerusalem

A.D. 53-57 Paul's third missionary journey

A.D. 52 Paul returns to Syrian Antioch

A.D. 50-51 To Galatia, Macedonia, Achaia

A.D. 50 Paul and Silas begin second missionary journey

A.D. 50 Jerusalem Council

A.D. 50 Conflicts over circumcision

A.D. 49-50 Paul writes Galatians?

A.D. 49-50 Paul and Barnabas return to Syrian Antioch

A.D. 49 Paul and Barnabas begin "first" missionary journey

A.D. 48 Paul and Barnabas to Jerusalem

A.D. 47 Barnabas to Syrian Antioch; with Paul at Tarsus

A.D. 38-48 Paul in Tarsus and region (est.)

A.D. 38 Paul meets Peter and James in Jerusalem

A.D. 35-38 Paul in Arabia, then Damascus

A.D. 35 Paul is converted on road to Damascus (est.)

A.D. 32 Paul arrests Jesus followers in Palestine (est.)

A.D. 16-22 Paul begins study in Jerusalem (est.)

5 B.C.-A.D.10 Paul is born (est.)

5 B.C. - A.D.10 Paul is Born (est.)

TWENTY YEARS HAD PASSED SINCE Paul, transformed by his conversion to Christ, had arrived in Jerusalem from Damascus. His reception by the apostles that year had understandably been cautious, one might even say icy. This was, after all, the arrogant young Pharisee who had approved the murder of Stephen and had gone from house to house arresting believers. Only because Barnabas had vouched for Paul's conversion did the church finally agree to receive him.

Much had happened in the intervening twenty years. Paul had traveled thousands of miles by land and sea, taking the gospel across the Roman Empire. He had founded churches, mentored the next generation of Christian leaders, and written half a dozen letters that would become the earliest written documents in the New Testament. He had profoundly shaped Christian theology and, though he had no way of knowing it, literally altered the future of Western civilization.

As Paul celebrated the successes of his ministry among the Gentiles, he also knew the costs that this effort had extracted from him. He offered a brief litany of these costs in his writings that became known as 2 Corinthians.

> I've faced death many times. I received the "forty lashes minus one" from the Jews five times. I was beaten with rods three times. I was stoned once. I was shipwrecked three times. I spent a day and a night on the open sea. I've been on many journeys. I faced dangers from rivers, robbers, my people, and Gentiles. I faced dangers in the city, in the desert, on the sea, and from false brothers and sisters. I faced these dangers with hard work and heavy labor, many sleepless nights, hunger and thirst, often without food, and in the cold without enough clothes. Besides all the other things I could mention, there's my daily stress because I'm concerned about all the churches. (2 Corinthians 11:23-28 CEB)

In spite of the costs, Paul never gave up. Among his defining characteristics were the dogged determination and perseverance that came from his conviction that the gospel "is the power of God for salvation to everyone who has faith, to the Jew first and also to the Greek" (Romans 1:16).

We see Paul's determination and willingness to suffer in how he faced the final chapter of his life. As Paul was traveling with his companions to bring the collection to Jerusalem, he was warned again and again that difficulties faced him there. His response to these warnings: "I am ready not only to be bound but even to die in Jerusalem for the name of the Lord Jesus" (Acts 21:13).

Arrival in Jerusalem

I've been to Jerusalem many times, and each time my heart beats faster. Jerusalem is at the center of the story that defines my life. Abraham and Isaac walked there. David made it his citadel. Solomon built his famous Temple there. The prophets offered words of warning and comfort regarding its fate. Jesus was born on its outskirts and was dedicated at the Temple, where later he cast out the moneychangers. Jesus entered the Holy City for his final week and was crucified there on a hill called Golgotha.

A rabbi friend of mine told me that when Jews enter Jerusalem, they feel a word deep in their soul: *home*. Surely Paul felt that way as he entered the city that late spring day in A.D. 57. His first stop was to meet with believers he knew. While breaking bread, he would have shared with them all that God had done in the previous four years. Luke appears to have been with him, listening as Paul recounted his time in Ephesus, his troubles with the church in Corinth, and the amazing spread of the gospel in Asia, Macedonia, and Greece. Paul's friends rejoiced in the exciting news.

The next day he went to meet with James and those whom Luke calls the "elders" of the Jerusalem church (21:18). Was Peter there? John? Who else may have been counted as an elder of the church? We don't know; only James is mentioned by name.

Ancient Roman street, Jerusalem

Paul and his companions would have presented to the elders the collection they had brought from the Gentile churches. It is curious that, although the offering clearly was important to Paul, Luke mentions it only in passing (Acts 24:17). As I read Luke's account of Paul's meeting with James, it makes me wonder if Paul came away disappointed that, after all the sacrifices of the Gentile believers, all the pressures Paul had exerted on them for the offering, and all the journeys Paul had made to collect it, James and the leaders seemed little affected by the gesture.

Instead, shortly after Paul described the success of his mission to the Gentiles, James or one of the other elders expressed the negative impression Jewish believers in Jerusalem had of Paul and what he had been teaching in Ephesus and beyond:

> "You see, brother, how many thousands of believers there are among the Jews, and they are all zealous for the law. They have been told about you that you teach all the Jews living among the Gentiles to forsake Moses, and that you tell them not to circumcise their children or observe the customs. What then is to be done? They will certainly hear that you have come." (Acts 21:20-22)

This statement is interesting for several reasons. First, it tells us that the gospel was making great inroads among the Jewish people, with "many thousands" of Jews having become believers, followers of Jesus whom they accepted as the Jewish Messiah. Second, the statement reveals that the Jewish believers were all "zealous for the law." This points to the rift that was developing between Paul's mission to the Gentiles and the mother church in Jerusalem.

Conflict with Church Leaders

With the urging of Paul and the support of Peter, the elders in Jerusalem had earlier conceded that Gentiles did not need to be circumcised nor follow most of the Law of Moses in order to be followers of Christ. But the church leaders apparently believed and taught that *Jewish* followers of Jesus were still to be circumcised and to obey the Law. There had been cases where Paul had gone along with that view when it was important to reach Jews, but he did not believe that God required Jews to obey the Law or be circumcised. In this, the believers in Jerusalem were right: Paul was neither as zealous for the Law as they were, nor did he insist that Jews obey the Law, follow the traditions, or have their children circumcised.

Paul describes his approach to the Law and reaching people for Christ in 1 Corinthians 9:20-22:

> To the Jews I became as a Jew, in order to win Jews. To those under the law I became as one under the law (though I myself am not under the law) so that I might win those under the law. To those outside the law I became as one outside the law (though I am not free from God's law but am under Christ's law) so that I might win those outside the law. To the weak I became weak, so that I might win the weak. I have become all things to all people, that I might by all means save some.

Though Paul may not have encouraged Jews to lay aside the Law, he did not believe that living under the Law was the basis of salvation. Paul believed that salvation—right standing with God; the blessings, love, and mercy of God; the gift of life now; and life eternal in God's kingdom—was a gift received only by faith.

It is worth pausing here to consider Paul's view of Scripture that was at the heart of the conflict between him and the Jewish believers. In Paul's time there was no single book that was the "Bible." The word does not appear in the New Testament. There were, instead, the "Scriptures" or "Scripture," from a Greek word meaning "writings." These were individual documents written on scrolls that the Jewish people considered authoritative. (The technology of binding sheets of paper into books was just beginning to be explored in the Greco-Roman world.)

Some groups, such as the Sadducees and Samaritans, considered only the Law of Moses to have binding authority, with the rest considered important ancient works but lacking the force of the Law. Other groups actually considered additional documents, besides the "books" of our Old Testament, to be Scripture as well. The most prominent of these groups was the Essenes, who produced the Dead Sea Scrolls. Found among the Dead Sea Scrolls were documents that the Essenes treated as Scripture, most of which did not have the force of Scripture among any other Jews.

The Pharisees considered most of the documents included in our Old Testament to be sacred Scripture—not only the Law, but also the Prophets and the Writings. Jews in Alexandria, Egypt, included some documents to be sacred Scripture that the Jews in Jerusalem ultimately rejected. These differences among the various collections of Scriptures are reflected today in the differences among the Old Testaments found in the Orthodox Church, the Roman Catholic Church, and the various Protestant churches.

Scripture and a New Covenant

When Paul wrote that "all scripture is inspired by God" (2 Timothy 3:16), I believe he meant that the three categories of Scripture embraced by the Pharisees and Essenes—the Law, the Prophets, and the Writings—were all inspired by God.* Christians have read a lot into that verse that Paul likely did not mean. In the verse, the Greek word for "inspired" is *theopneustos*. Curiously, prior to that time, it appears nowhere else in the Bible and nowhere else in the Greek language that we know of; it may be that Paul created this word as a metaphor for the Scripture's authority. It is a combination of two words: *theo*, which means God; and *pneustos*, from the root *pneuma*, which means wind, breath, or spirit.

This word has occasionally been interpreted to mean something akin to God-dictated, but it seems more likely to mean that in some way (Paul does not feel the need to explain how) God has breathed upon the human authors of Scripture or upon the Scriptures they wrote, making the Law, the Prophets, and the Writings "useful for teaching, for showing mistakes, for correcting, and for training character" (2 Timothy 3:16 CEB).

Paul looked at the Law, the one section of the Scriptures that traditionally all Jews agreed had the force of binding authority, and he taught that it no longer was binding but now served as a guide—that is, God's people were no longer required to follow it as law but rather to see in it principles and precepts that might equip them "for every good work" (2 Timothy 3:17). It was precisely this understanding of the Scriptures that allowed Paul to set aside the command for circumcision, which predated the Law. It was this view of Scripture that allowed him, as a Jew *and* a follower of Jesus, to eat foods the Law considered unclean.

In 2 Corinthians 3, Paul uses the language of covenant to describe what Jesus did. As noted previously, Jesus brought

* Most mainline scholars believe that a disciple of Paul wrote 2 Timothy, attempting to restate Paul's thinking for a later generation.

a new covenant, a new binding agreement between God and humanity. This new covenant was foretold by God through Jeremiah when, six hundred years before the time of Christ, he wrote, "The days are surely coming, says the LORD, when I will make a new covenant with the house of Israel and the house of Judah" (Jeremiah 31:31). Jesus spoke of it when he took the wine at the Last Supper and called it "the new covenant in my blood" (Luke 22:20).

The previous covenant had been made with Israel through Moses, and its terms had been expressed in the Law. That previous covenant said that if God's people would obey the Law, then God would be their God and they would be his people. In other words, righteousness was defined by obedience to the Law. But Paul proclaims that in Jesus' gospel, "the righteousness of God is revealed through faith for faith; as it is written, 'The one who is righteous will live by faith'" (Romans 1:17). For Paul, God had made a new covenant with humanity, both Jew and Gentile, in which salvation was received by faith and offered as pure gift, in response to which believers would seek to live in such a way as to please God.

Several years ago, my wife, LaVon, and I refinanced our house. We had been paying 6.75 percent interest, a good rate when we had bought the house seven years earlier, but we were able to refinance at 3.75 percent. Our mortgage was a covenant, a binding agreement between ourselves and the lender. When we closed on the new loan, we entered into a new covenant. At that time our original mortgage was paid off, and the previous agreement we had made was completely satisfied. The old covenant (mortgage) was no longer binding upon us. We now had a new covenant with different terms. Similarly, God had entered into a covenant with Israel, promising to be Israel's God and they his people. But in Jesus Christ, a new covenant was initiated by God with humanity. Christians remember this covenant and its terms each time we share the Eucharist and recall Jesus' words, "This is my blood of the new covenant…"

This comparison of biblical covenants and contemporary home mortgages, like any analogy, eventually breaks down. However, I think the comparison is helpful in following the somewhat complex theological argument Paul makes in several of his epistles regarding Christ's salvation and the Christian's relationship to the Law.

Discord in the Temple

When James and the elders Paul met with told him the Jewish believers in Jerusalem were "zealous for the Law," it was clear that Paul and the Jewish believers in Jerusalem held very different views of the relationship of, at the very least, the Jewish believer to the Law. But we know that many of the Jewish believers continued to feel that Gentiles needed to abide by some or perhaps all of the Law as well. This is why some among the Jewish believers had followed after Paul in the mission field, attempting to correct Paul's teaching concerning circumcision.

The elders wanted Paul to demonstrate his commitment to the Law. Here is what the elders told Paul he should do to prove he still lived according to the Law: "You must therefore do what we tell you. Four men among us have made a solemn promise. Take them with you, go through the purification ritual with them, and pay the cost of having their heads shaved. Everyone will know there is nothing to those reports about you but that you too live a life in keeping with the Law" (Acts 21:23-24 CEB).

In other words, the elders wanted Paul to publicly observe some part of the Law or tradition. (Scholars disagree about exactly what all these terms meant, but they agree the terms were intended to prove that Paul was still a faithful Jew.) Surprisingly, Paul went along with the terms, recognizing perhaps that failing to do so could stir up a great deal of trouble for the mother church, or perhaps hoping to win the elders' support for his missionary efforts.

Jerusalem. The Temple once stood where the Muslim Dome of the Rock stands today.

The elders' plan did not accomplish what they had hoped. Instead, while Paul was in the Temple, Jews from Asia (presumably Ephesus) recognized him and began shouting in the courts, "Fellow Israelites, help! This is the man who is teaching everyone everywhere against our people, our Law, and this place" (Acts 21:28). They also accused Paul of bringing Greeks (Gentiles) into the inner courts of the Temple. Gentiles were allowed in the Temple courts, in an outer area called the Court of the Gentiles, but the area nearer the Holy of Holies was reserved for Jews. Signs were posted all around the short wall that separated these areas, warning that Gentiles entering the inner courts would be put to death. Though Paul had not in fact brought Greeks into the inner courts, his association with the Greeks had led the Jews from Ephesus to assume he had. Further, his view of the Law, taught openly in Ephesus for nearly three years, was seen by these Jews as teaching "against our people, our Law, and this place."

The angry response of the crowd upon hearing these accusations was similar to the response of the people in Ephesus when they had heard Paul was teaching against Artemis and her temple: "Then all the city was aroused, and the people rushed together. They seized Paul and dragged him out of the temple" (21:30). In their rage they would have killed him for such blasphemy.

Paul's experience, like the experience in Ephesus, points to one of the challenges of religious belief: passionate, deeply held convictions, if not tempered by Jesus' call to love neighbors and enemies, can lead religious people to act in horribly irreligious ways in order to protect the honor of their gods.

The Crusades were fueled by this same kind of religious passion, and it led followers of Jesus to do the exact opposite of what he had taught. Similarly, recent attacks of Muslim extremists on those they perceive to be insulting the Prophet cause them to do the opposite of Muhammad's teachings.

Paul might have been killed that day were it not for the quick response of the Roman soldiers who, from the walls of the Fortress Antonia adjacent to the Temple, looked down on the Temple courts, watching for anything that looked like violence or rebellion. Seeing the outbreak, soldiers rushed in to find out what was happening and arrested Paul, as much to protect him as to stop the violence. I encourage the reader to follow the story in Acts 21:27–22:29. In it, as Paul is taken away by the Romans, he is allowed to speak to the crowd from the steps, giving the first of two lengthy testimonies about how he came to faith in Christ. (The second took place while he was on trial before King Agrippa II in Acts 26.)

Paul's Testimony and Ours

We've seen examples of Paul's testimony previously. Undoubtedly he often shared the testimony of his conversion experience and how life was different after he answered Christ's call to follow. What stands out to me about the two times Paul shared his witness in Acts, and the way he regularly refers to his own faith and experiences of God's grace in his letters, is the power of personal testimony, for Paul and for us.

Some years ago in worship I asked our members to write down their faith story, their witness or testimony, by answering several questions:

- How and when did you become a Christian?
- What led you to become a Christian?
- How have you experienced God working in your life?
- How has being a Christian positively changed your life?

My experience in conversations with atheists (I'm having a couple of these right now on social media) is that it's impossible to win an argument with them, nor are they likely to win an argument with me. For every argument I can make for the existence of God, they have a counterargument. For every argument they make, I have a counterargument. In the end, after all the reasons are exhausted, the most compelling case I can make for my faith comes from my experience of God and the ways that my life is different as a Christ-follower from what it was before I came to follow him. This is my personal witness or testimony.

As Paul stood before the crowd that day on the steps of the Fortress Antonia, he shared his testimony. He did not offer rational arguments for why Jesus was the long-awaited Jewish messiah. He did not speak of justification by faith or any other theological concept found in his epistles. He simply shared the story of how he had persecuted the followers of the Way, even to their death, and how one day on the road to Damascus, Christ had spoken to him, and he had seen the light—quite literally. In that moment, the man who had been the leading persecutor of the Way became its biggest proponent.

In Acts 22–26, Luke records at least five different "trials" in which Paul testified to his faith before his adversaries. There is his testimony before the crowd on the steps of the fortress. The next day he was brought before the Sanhedrin, the council that Paul likely once aspired to join, where with boldness he gave a testimony that ended in an uproar, with the Roman soldiers once more having to save him. The next evening, when a plot by Jewish leaders to kill Paul was discovered, he was transferred by night to Caesarea by the Sea. There, five days later, Paul gave his defense before the Roman governor of Judea, Antonius Felix. Two years later Paul would offer his defense before Antonius Felix's successor, Porcius Festus, and still later before King Agrippa II. Years later, in a hearing not recorded in Acts, Paul would give his testimony once more before a court in Rome.

Setting the Context

As you read Paul's story in Acts, keep in mind the historical context in which Luke wrote the Book of Acts and how that context may have affected his telling of the story.

Most scholars agree that Acts was written in the years after the Romans destroyed Jerusalem in response to what is called the "first Jewish revolt." The revolt began in A.D. 66, at which time the rebels experienced several quick and remarkable victories over the Romans. In response, Rome unleashed four legions on the inhabitants of the Holy Land. The first-century Jewish historian Josephus records that by A.D. 73, when the last of the rebellion was put down at Masada, over a million Jews had died and Jerusalem had been completely destroyed. Nearly another hundred thousand Jews were taken to Rome as slaves.

Luke appears to have been writing primarily for a Gentile audience within the Roman Empire in the years following the Jewish revolt. After the seven-year war with the Jews of Palestine, why would non-Jews be interested in embracing a Jewish religion? The Gospel of Luke paints a picture of Jesus Christ that was compelling to the Gentile world, including Jesus' concern for the poor, the outsiders, and the nobodies; Jesus' conflict with the Jewish leadership that resulted in his death; and ultimately his triumph over death.

Similarly, Luke's telling of Paul's story in Acts emphasizes God's concern for the Gentiles and Paul's own struggle with "the Jews," who repeatedly sought to kill him. Luke also records several times when Roman soldiers saved Paul, and he describes the conversion of a Roman soldier under Peter's ministry. By presenting the story in this way, Luke's account in Acts emphasizes Paul's Roman citizenship. Luke makes clear that the Way, though emerging from within Judaism, was not synonymous with Judaism and in every city was embraced by many Gentiles.

Prison Again

As noted above, Paul was transferred from Jerusalem to a town called Caesarea by the Sea (often called Caesarea Maritima to distinguish it from Caesarea Philippi, located sixty miles to the northeast). This magnificent city, built by Herod the Great between 25 and 13 B.C., was both beautiful and an amazing engineering feet. Herod built a man-made harbor on the Mediterranean Sea, then constructed a palace, a temple dedicated to the Roman emperor, a large amphitheater, a hippodrome (a track for racing horses and chariots), and a host of other buildings, the remains of which can still be explored at the archaeological site in Israel, not far from Tel Aviv. Guides there sometimes point out a location among the ruins that is said to be the prison cell of Paul. This is not likely, but it does remind visitors that Paul spent two years in prison there.

Luke tells us that governor Antonius Felix, in ruling about how to handle Paul, "ordered the centurion to keep him in custody, but to let him have some liberty and not to prevent any of his friends from taking care of his needs" (Acts 24:23). During Paul's two-year imprisonment in Caesarea, it seems likely that Paul had no shortage of friends who met with, encouraged, and provided for him. One was Philip the Evangelist, a deacon in the early church. Paul had stayed with Philip and his family on the way to Jerusalem a short time before being arrested. Another may have been Cornelius, a Roman centurion stationed in Caesarea, a Gentile whom Peter had led to Christ. The story

Caesarea Maritima

of Cornelius is pivotal in Acts and was instrumental in shaping the church's thinking about Gentiles. It's easy to imagine him providing encouragement and help to meet Paul's physical needs. It seems likely that in prison Paul would have composed letters to the various churches he had founded, though most of these letters have likely been lost. Some have argued that Philemon, Colossians, and Ephesians may have been written during that time.*

At the end of two years, Antonius Felix was replaced by Porcius Festus as the Roman governor of Judea. It is thought that Festus became governor around A.D. 59 or 60, which aligns with the chronology I've been suggesting. When Festus assumed office, the Jewish leadership in Jerusalem petitioned him to have Paul transferred back to Jerusalem. (Luke tells us

* For one example of the case for Paul writing these letters from Caesarea see Bo Reicke, "Caesarea, Rome, and the Captivity Epistles," in *Apostolic History and the Gospel: Biblical and Historical Essays Presented to F.F. Bruce*, ed. W. Ward Gasque and Ralph P. Martin (Exeter: Paternoster Press, 1970), 277-86. (ISBN: 085364098X).

they planned to kill Paul on the return trip). Festus asked Paul's accusers to travel to Caesarea and make their case to him there. In that trial, the Jewish leaders once again brought serious charges against Paul and asked that he be sent to Jerusalem. When Festus asked Paul if he was willing to face his accusers in Jerusalem, Paul appealed his case to Rome, as was his right as a Roman citizen.

Several days after Paul's appeal, King Agrippa II and his sister Bernice came to Caesarea to welcome Festus as the new governor of Judea. The thirty-two-year-old king, the last of Herod's line, was a Jew who had been educated in Rome, was known as a friend of Romans, and was appointed by the emperor to serve as king of a territory that spanned much of the Galilee, the Golan Heights, and what today is southern Syria.

When Agrippa and Bernice arrived in Caesarea, Festus described Paul's case, and Agrippa indicated he wanted to hear Paul himself. Thus Paul was given one more chance to share his testimony, this time not only before a Roman governor, but before a man who would be the last king of his own people.

Upon hearing Paul's testimony, King Agrippa declared, "This man is doing nothing to deserve death or imprisonment" (Acts 26:32). It seems likely to me that Luke included Agrippa's statement as a way of demonstrating to his Gentile readers that Paul, in the eyes of this friend of Rome, was blameless.*

Journey to Rome

And so, after two years in prison, after testifying before two Roman governors and King Agrippa II, Paul was sent off to Rome to stand trial before the emperor's court. We know that Paul had

* The King James Version of Agrippa's response to Paul reads, "Almost thou persuadest me to be a Christian." (Acts 26:28) This was the text for one of John Wesley's most famous sermons, "The Almost Christian," a sermon he preached at Oxford in 1741 in which he noted that many people are "almost Christian," yet he called his hearers that day to become not merely almost Christians, but all-together Christians.

hoped to travel to Rome, something he had indicated two years earlier in his letter to the Roman believers, so it's not hard to imagine how Paul felt about the trip. He had always intended to go to Rome, but now, thanks to the accusations of his fellow Jews, Rome would foot the bill for his journey!

The year was likely A.D. 59 or perhaps 60. The journey was just shy of two thousand miles. Under the best of conditions it would take a month, allowing for stops at ports along the way. But Paul's journey, as we will see, took far longer.

Paul was joined on the trip by Luke and a disciple named Aristarchus, who is described in Colossians as Paul's "fellow prisoner." Luke uses the first-person plural throughout his account of the voyage to Rome, apparently wanting the reader to know he was along on the journey.* Indeed, the detailed information in Luke's account is consistent with that of an eyewitness: we learn the name of Paul's Roman guard, the guard's regiment, the ship, the seaports where they landed, and other details that could be easily checked against known facts, even twenty years after the events he describes.

Luke's account of the journey certainly is dramatic, but I believe its primary intent is to help us learn about Paul's life

* As noted earlier, some critical scholars suggest that use of the first-person plural was to give the account a stronger sense of authenticity, noting that this literary technique was occasionally used by authors who had not been on the journey they described. Perhaps, but two things mitigate against this in my mind: First, Luke is writing as a follower of Jesus Christ who it would seem would not be inclined to write suggesting he was on an important journey he was not actually on. And second, the description of Paul's journey to Rome is so detailed, with accurate knowledge of ports, names of people and ships, yet Luke does not include such detail elsewhere in Acts. What possible reason would he have to begin using this level of detail at this point in the Gospel while not using it earlier? Some scholars suggest Luke was merely incorporating first-person material taken from another source. Perhaps, but it seems likely that there were other first-person accounts he had access to for his Gospel and for material in the first part of Acts, but he does not incorporate the first-person plural in those places. I'm not opposed to believing that Luke used this literary device; it just seems to be a less likely explanation for the account of the journey. My own conclusion is that Luke was on this journey with Paul.

and faith. In places, the account resembles Homer's epic story of Odysseus, a similarity that may have been intended to emphasize Paul's heroism.

In Paul's day, ships often avoided sailing in the open sea, preferring instead to stay as near as possible to land, which was safer and which allowed for regular stops at ports to load and unload cargo and passengers. The first part of Paul's journey bears this out (see map).

It was mid-September when Paul and his companions sailed from Caesarea to Myra, where they changed ships and set out for Rome. At that time of year the strong winds would have begun, making sea travel more difficult and gradually increasing until mid-November, when sailing generally ceased and did not pick up again until early spring.

Luke's account of the journey shows the voyage becoming more precarious with each passing day. He notes that "the winds were against us," then later writes, "We sailed slowly for a number of days and arrived with difficulty off Cnidus" (Acts 27:4,7). Next he notes, "Much time had been lost, and sailing had already become dangerous because by now it was after the Day of Atonement" (27:9 NIV). That would have been October 5 in the year 59, well into the dangerous season and making it highly unlikely that the ship could arrive in Rome before sailing was called off for the winter.

At that point Paul warned the captain, crew, and his Roman captor, "Sirs, I can see that the voyage will be with danger and much heavy loss, not only of the cargo and the ship, but also of our lives" (27:10). Paul had reason to speak up. In 2 Corinthians 11:25, he tells the church at Corinth in a letter written prior to this journey, "Three times I was shipwrecked; for a night and a day I was adrift at sea." He was about to experience a fourth shipwreck.

The captain, captors, and crew dismissed Paul's advice and decided to set sail for points farther west. This proved disastrous. As they sailed from Crete, a tremendous storm came up, the kind of storm that often destroyed ships such as theirs. Luke writes, "We were being pounded by the storm so violently that on the next day they began to throw the cargo overboard, and on the third day with their own hands they threw the ship's tackle overboard. When neither sun nor stars appeared for many days, and no small tempest raged, all hope of our being saved was at last abandoned" (Acts 27:18-20).

This storm at sea is reminiscent of another in the masterpiece of ancient Hebrew literature, Jonah. The account of Paul's journey to Rome and Jonah's experience at sea are about the same length: Paul's is sixty verses, Jonah's forty-eight. Both take their lead characters to the capital city of an empire that threatens God's people. Both proclaim God's judgment and mercy in those cities. But while Jonah is forever identified as one who resisted God's call to preach in Nineveh, Paul devoted his life to pursuing God's call and longed to share the good news in Rome.

The Prisoner Preaches

Earlier in Paul's journey to Rome, he had urged the captain and crew to winter on the island of Crete, rather than continuing to risk travel in the storms. Now, with their ship blown hundreds of miles off course, Paul told them,

> "Men, you should have listened to me and not have set sail from Crete and thereby avoided this damage and loss. I urge you now to keep up your courage, for there will be no loss of life among you, but only of the ship. For last night there stood by me an angel of the God to whom I belong and whom I worship, and he said, 'Do not be afraid, Paul; you must stand before the emperor; and indeed, God has granted safety to all those who are sailing with you.' So keep up your courage, men, for I have faith in God that it will be exactly as I have been told. But we will have to run aground on some island." (Acts 27:21-26)

Paul was boldly preaching hope to the soldiers, sailors, and his fellow passengers, 276 people in all. What an interesting dynamic: Paul the prisoner was also Paul the preacher proclaiming God's deliverance and salvation to those aboard the ship. He promised that the Lord would deliver them. In this, once more, there are parallels with Jonah, who proclaimed God's deliverance to his shipmates, though in Jonah's case deliverance came when they threw him overboard. Both Paul and Jonah were instruments used by God to calm the storm and to deliver their shipmates.

Paul's ship finally struck a sandbar just off the coast of Malta, a small island about eight miles wide and eighteen miles long. There is an inlet on the northern coast of Malta known as St. Paul's Bay, which may well have been where this story took place. The ship was torn apart by the waves, but every person aboard made it safely it to shore just as Paul had promised.

Once on shore, the natives of the island "showed us unusual kindness" (Acts 28:2), building a fire and welcoming sailors and prisoners alike. Paul, helping to collect wood for the fire, was bitten by a poisonous snake, yet he did not die or show any sign of ill health from the bite. Seeing this, the people proclaimed

St. Paul's Bay, Malta

that Paul was a god! It was the first miracle associated with Paul on Malta, but it would not be the last.

Paul and the rest of his shipmates were welcomed to the estate of a man named Publius, the leading citizen of Malta, who housed them for three days while arrangements could be made to determine which residents in Malta would take persons into their homes. While there, Paul prayed for Publius's father, who had been sick with dysentery, and the man was healed. Soon all those on the island who were sick began coming to Paul. He prayed for them, and they were made well.

Paul and his companions were in Malta for three months, during which Luke notes once more the hospitality and kindness of the Maltese people: "They bestowed many honors on us, and when we were about to sail, they put on board all the provisions we needed" (Acts 28:10).

Had the people of Malta become Christian during these three months? Many, inspired by Paul, undoubtedly had. Yet even prior to Paul's preaching, these natives had demonstrated kindness and hospitality toward strangers, soldiers, and even prisoners.

It is interesting that in the story of Paul's journey to Rome, nonbelievers consistently showed kindness to Paul, and in this case to his shipmates as well. Paul's guard, Julius, was kind to Paul again and again, even saving Paul's life. The people of Malta showed extraordinary kindness to Paul and the others on the ship. Publius showed great hospitality to those who had been stranded.

The kind treatment of Paul by non-Christians brings to mind several passages in Romans that point us toward Paul's view of Gentiles who did not know Christ yet lived as though they did. In Romans 1:20, Paul notes that God's power and divine nature are clearly seen in creation, so that all people have access to some knowledge of God. This knowledge is written on our hearts, so all of us—believers and nonbelievers—have at least some common and basic sense of right and wrong.

I recently participated in a panel discussion on evangelism at Africa University in Zimbabwe. One of my fellow panelists was Professor John Kurewa, the E. Stanley Jones Professor of Evangelism at Africa University. He noted that the missionaries who came to Africa in centuries past believed they were bringing God to the Africans. But Dr. Kurewa noted that God was already in Africa prior to the arrival of the missionaries. He pointed out that the Africans knew God and sought to follow God and to do God's will as they understood it. What the missionaries brought was the good news of Jesus.

Paul writes of this distinction in Romans 2 and offers some interesting insights, noting that God will "give eternal life to those who look for glory, honor, and immortality based on their patient good work" (v. 7 CEB) and that,

> It isn't the ones who hear the Law who are righteous in God's eyes. It is the ones who do what the Law says who will be treated as righteous. Gentiles don't have the Law. But when they instinctively do what the Law requires they are a Law in themselves, though they don't have the Law. They show the proof of the Law written on their hearts, and their consciences affirm it. Their conflicting thoughts will accuse them, or even make a defense for them, on the day when, according to my gospel, God will judge the hidden truth about human beings through Christ Jesus. (Romans 2:13-16 CEB)

Scholars debate the meaning of these words. Paul's arguments regarding salvation in this passage are subtle, and his logic is not always easy to discern. But I hear in Paul's words his experience of Gentiles who knew neither the Law nor Jesus Christ, yet knew God and instinctively responded to the Law that was written on their hearts by God. I mention this because I'm often asked about the eternal fate of people who are not Christians. Many have been taught that people who do not personally receive Jesus Christ as their Lord and Savior will spend eternity in hell. Paul's writings and theology are more nuanced than that and seem to leave room for alternative answers to the eternal fate of nonbelievers.*

Resuming the Journey

Finally, when after three months the weather and winds were amenable to sailing, Paul and his companions boarded a ship that had wintered in Malta and set out again for Rome. In another week they were at the port city of Puteoli, where they disembarked. Paul, his friends, and Julius his centurion guard were welcomed into the home of believers in Puteoli, undoubtedly much better accommodations than would otherwise have been arranged by Julius. By that time it was clear that Julius had become more than a guard who was escorting Paul to Rome; one wonders if he had not by then become a follower of Jesus as well.

The journey from Puteoli to Rome was one hundred forty-two miles and would have taken another week to ten days, during which time Paul was greeted by two other groups of Christians—one group that met him at the Forum of Appius, forty miles south of Rome, and another group that joined him at the Three Taverns, thirty miles from Rome. So, with Luke, Aristarchus, Julius, and a large gathering of friends to accompany him, Paul continued to Rome.

What a surprising scene this must have been for Julius, a kind of triumphal entry in which Paul the prisoner was met with expressions of love and affection by the crowd. Finally Paul—with his friends at his side, and after a five- to six-month journey that included terrifying storms, a shipwreck, the bite of a viper, and a winter stay healing and evangelizing on Malta—arrived at his destination, the center of the Roman Empire. At long last he was in Rome.

---

* I've written about this subject in *Christianity and World Religions* (Nashville: Abingdon, 2005).

As mentioned before, I worked on this book while on a plane home from southern Africa. Our church has partnered with multiple churches and missions in Africa. I was visiting to offer encouragement, see the projects we've supported, teach and be taught, and discern what our church is being called to do in support of our Christian brothers and sisters in South Africa, Malawi, and Zimbabwe during the years ahead.

In all honesty, the trip to Africa had not been pleasant. It took three planes and twenty-eight hours of flights and layovers to get to Malawi. We flew coach, and the seats on international flights always seem even closer together than on the domestic flights. I never can sleep when flying across the Atlantic, even if I take a sleeping pill. By the time I got off the plane in Africa, I thought to myself, as I often do after such trips, *Never again*.

Then I thought of Paul. His trips weren't twenty-eight hours by air; they were months and months by ship and by land. He didn't have pillows and blankets and flight attendants bringing meals and water every few hours. He didn't land safely in each city but was shipwrecked and lost at sea on multiple occasions. At most my fitness bracelet registered fifteen thousand steps walked in a day, but Paul routinely walked more than thirty thousand steps while carrying his accommodations on his back.

On my way home from Africa, my heart was filled once again with gratitude and awe at the opportunity to be with believers in Africa, to see the ministries and mission, and to hear the stories of lives that have been changed. I know I will be back. Realizing this, I'm embarrassed at how little I'm willing to suffer before I start thinking *Never again*, particularly compared with Paul's ministry.

I'm also reminded that what Paul attempted and accomplished can't be described any other way than by the word *call*. Paul felt called by God to go on his journeys, and he was willing to face illness, persecution, prison, and death to fulfill that call.

Rome

Paul arrived in Rome in the spring of A.D. 60. Though he had never been to Rome, he already had many friends there. His epistle to the Christians at Rome, written from Corinth several years earlier, closes with Paul sending greetings to twenty-six people he names and many others that are unnamed. Most of these people appear to have been leaders of the church in Rome. The twenty-six he names were friends and in some cases family members of Paul.

One thing that stands out in this list is the large number of women. In spite of Paul's instructions elsewhere about women in the church remaining silent, many of the women he names here seem to have been key figures in the church, including a deacon, a fellow prisoner, and a woman named Mary who had worked "very hard" for the believers in Rome.

Not only by his letter to the Romans, but also through his reputation, influence, and impact among the Gentiles, Paul was well known to the believers in Rome long before he arrived there in the spring of 60.

Based on what Paul writes in Romans 16, there seem to have been multiple house churches in Rome by the mid-50s. Several years later, when he finally arrived there, the number undoubtedly had expanded.

Paul explicitly names one church that was meeting in the home of Priscilla and Aquila. We first met the couple in Corinth, where ten years earlier Paul had joined them in tentmaking while encouraging their continued growth in faith. He had taken them with him to Ephesus at the end of his second missionary journey, asking them to begin laying the groundwork for the gospel in anticipation of his return to Ephesus on his third missionary journey. It seems likely that, after arriving in Ephesus on his third journey, Paul then had sent the couple to Rome.

St. Paul Regalo, the church built atop the place claimed to have been where Paul was kept under house arrest for at least two years in Rome

When Paul arrived in Rome, he was allowed to "live by himself, with the soldier who was guarding him" (Acts 28:16). In Ephesians 6:20, he mentions that he was "in chains for the sake of the gospel" (CEB). Was he literally shackled during those two years, or were the "chains" a metaphor for being under house arrest? We don't know. In Rome, at the Basilica of Saint Paul Outside the Walls, a church built atop what is believed to be the burial place of Paul, chains are on display that are said to have shackled Paul at some point during his imprisonment.*

In Rome, churches often were built atop places traditionally associated with events in the lives of the Apostles Peter and Paul. In the video that is available as a companion to this book, I take viewers to some of those churches, recounting Paul's final days by visiting them. One of the churches is San Paolo alla Regola. It is not part of the standard tours of Rome, and

*While I'm a bit of a skeptic when it comes to these kind of relics, doubtful that in most cases things like the chains of Paul survived, I don't discount entirely that these could have been used on Paul. Regardless, they do serve as a visible reminder of the fact that at some point Paul would have been literally chained.

in fact my guide was unfamiliar with it. The church is one of two churches that may have been associated with Paul's house arrest (the other being Santa Maria in Via Lata). Under the church are the remains of a far more ancient building said to have been the house where Paul lived. It is impossible to know if this and other churches associated with Paul are in fact the actual locations of these events, but they serve as markers for telling the story. During our time in Rome we retraced Paul's journey from his house arrest to his beheading to his burial by visiting the churches associated with each of those events.

The Christians at Rome likely had arranged for the house Paul rented. Once there, among the first things Paul did was meet with the leaders of the Jewish community. We learn in Acts that three days after arriving in Rome, Paul called the Jewish leaders together, and they agreed that he should have a chance to address others in the Jewish community. Paul met with them at the house for several days, where

> From morning until evening he explained the matter to them, testifying to the kingdom of God and trying to convince them about Jesus both from the law of Moses and from the prophets. Some were convinced by what he had said, while others refused to believe. (Acts 28:23-24)

To end his time with the Jewish leaders and others who had come to hear him, Paul offered a quotation from Scripture that indicated his frustration with those Jews who refused to believe. He quoted Isaiah 6:9-11, in which God called Isaiah to preach to the Israelites but warned Isaiah that they would not listen. By quoting this Scripture, Paul was in effect criticizing those Jewish people who refused to hear, repent, and be saved. Paul then repeated the words that got him into trouble in Jerusalem: "Let it be known to you then that this salvation of God has been sent to the Gentiles; they will listen" (Acts 28:28).*

* Some of the early texts of Acts do not have this statement.

Two Mysteries

Following Paul's statement, the Book of Acts abruptly ends with these words: "He lived there two whole years at his own expense and welcomed all who came to him, proclaiming the kingdom of God and teaching about the Lord Jesus Christ with all boldness and without hindrance" (vv. 30-31).

Scholars have been perplexed by this ending for two reasons. The first is why, since Acts was written when Paul was no longer alive, Luke would not tell the story of the apostle's death. No one knows the answer, but over the years scholars have come up with various theories. Here's what I think: though Theophilus (presumably the literary patron who commissioned Luke to write Luke and Acts*) and all the early readers of Acts would know how Paul met his end, Luke wanted them to remember Paul as a remarkable and heroic man who did what God called him to do—teaching, preaching, and making disciples, even when he was under house arrest.

I am reminded of funerals where families choose to have a closed casket. Often a family member will say, "I want to remember my loved one as they were in life, not as they were in death." Likewise in most eulogies I give at funerals, the focus is on the good things the people did while they were alive, not on how and when they died. Seen in this way, we might say the latter half of Acts is Luke's eulogy for Paul.

The second reason scholars have been perplexed by the ending is even more immediate than the issue of Paul's death. Acts ends with Paul under house arrest, awaiting trial. What was the outcome of that trial? The tradition in the early church was that Paul died around A.D. 64 or 65, about the same time Peter died. The emperor Nero began persecuting Christians, making

* Some believe Theophilus is simply a representative name for all who would read Luke's work—the name means "lover of God" and it is possible Luke was writing to all lovers of God who were followers of Jesus. But knowing that historians often did their work with the help of patrons who commissioned their histories, it seems likely to me that Luke was writing for a man named Theophilus.

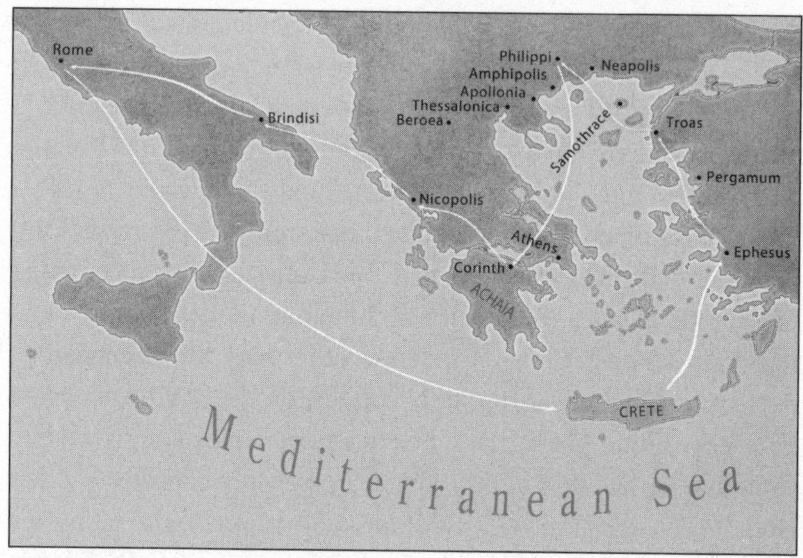

Map of Paul's possible "fourth" journey

them scapegoats for the Great Fire of Rome (more about this shortly). If Paul came to Rome in A.D. 60, and Luke tells us he was kept under house arrest for two years, taking us to A.D. 62, then what happened between A.D. 62 and A.D. 64 or 65? If Paul had been released and had pursued a fourth missionary journey, we would have expected Luke to narrate that journey as well, given that most scholars believe Luke wrote at least a decade or two after Paul's death.

One theory can be found in the Letters of Titus and 1 and 2 Timothy, usually called the "Pastoral Epistles." If taken at face value, these letters were written by Paul and were based on his having been acquitted at the end of the two years of house arrest described in Acts. The letters seem to indicate that Paul then embarked on a fourth missionary journey, after which he was arrested and imprisoned and tried in Rome for a second time. According to this view, the letters date from the period between the acquittal and the second arrest and trial. In fact, 2 Timothy claims to be written by Paul from prison in Rome as Paul anticipates his death.

We can piece together some of the locations Paul may have visited on a fourth missionary journey from places mentioned in the letters. First Timothy mentions a visit of Paul to Ephesus and a subsequent visit to Macedonia (a region that includes Philippi and Thessalonica as well as others). This would indicate that a fourth missionary journey involved revisiting the churches Paul had founded on his second and third missionary journeys, at least those along the Aegean Sea. In addition, the letter to Titus has Paul visiting Crete, a journey otherwise not recorded in Acts. It has Paul wintering in Nicopolis, on the northwest coast of Greece along the Adriatic Sea, a city and area not previously visited in earlier missionary journeys. Second Timothy, written after Paul's arrest and second imprisonment in Rome, mentions visits to Corinth and Miletus. It also mentions that Paul left a coat in Troas. From these clues we might piece together a missionary journey that would have Paul leaving Rome and going to Crete, Miletus, Ephesus, Troas, Philippi, Thessalonica, Corinth, and then to Nicopolis before returning to Rome. (Some early church traditions also suggest Paul visited Spain as a part of his fourth missionary journey.)

This fourth missionary journey is called into question by the fact that a great number of scholars today believe that the Pastoral Epistles were written decades after Paul's death, by those who followed and loved Paul and who sought to give him voice and to recount his story for a later generation. According to this view, the Pastoral Epistles may contain fragments of letters Paul actually wrote or accurate traditions about Paul, but the themes, vocabulary, and setting behind the letters seem to be a better fit for the period in the late first or early second century, long after Paul's death. I'll leave readers to explore on their own the arguments for a fourth missionary journey, as well as the debate about the authenticity of the Pastoral Epistles.

Final Years

Whether Paul was acquitted at the end of the two years described in Acts or remained in prison until his death, we know that he continued to preach, teach, and write letters during the final years of his life. Philippians, Ephesians, Colossians, and Philemon, known as the Prison Epistles, all clearly state that Paul was in prison or in chains when he wrote them.* We don't know if all these letters were written from Rome, but it is likely that some were.

Among my favorite letters of Paul is his Epistle to the Philippians. It is known as Paul's "epistle of joy," because the tone is one of rejoicing, and it calls for rejoicing in response. It is a thank-you letter written to the church at Philippi for a gift they sent by the hands of one of their members. In reply Paul tells them, "I now have plenty and it is more than enough. I am full to overflowing because I received the gifts that you sent from Epaphroditus" (Philippians 4:18 CEB).

Philippians sheds light on what Paul is experiencing and how he faces his imprisonment and the possibility of death. Among the most loved passages in this epistle, made all the more remarkable because it was likely written during his house arrest in Rome, is Philippians 4:4-7:

> Rejoice in the Lord always; again I will say, Rejoice. Let your gentleness be known to everyone. The Lord is near. Do not worry about anything, but in everything by prayer and supplication with thanksgiving let your requests be made known to God. And the peace of God, which surpasses all understanding, will guard your hearts and your minds in Christ Jesus.

* As with the Pastoral Epistles, some question the authorship of Ephesians and Colossians and to a lesser degree, Philemon. Most agree that Paul wrote Philippians. When I read these I assume Paul wrote them or that someone close to Paul took his ideas and edited these. In addition to the authorship debate, there is debate about where Paul was imprisoned when writing these letters.

As with his first imprisonment while in Philippi, here again Paul faces hardship and imprisonment with faith and hope and as a result experiences the peace that passes all understanding.

Throughout the letter he demonstrates this same confidence and hope. He views his imprisonment as providential, because by it he has been able to proclaim the gospel to the emperor's guards. He believes his imprisonment has furthered the gospel and evoked greater boldness on the part of Christians everywhere who know he suffers for the gospel. And he speaks frankly about the possibility that the trial might result in his death:

> It is my eager expectation and hope that I will not be put to shame in any way, but that by my speaking with all boldness, Christ will be exalted now as always in my body, whether by life or by death. For to me, living is Christ and dying is gain. If I am to live in the flesh, that means fruitful labor for me; and I do not know which I prefer. I am hard pressed between the two: my desire is to depart and be with Christ, for that is far better; but to remain in the flesh is more necessary for you.
>
> (Philippians 1:20-24)

I have often recommended that those who are dying meditate upon the words of Paul's letter to the Philippians, slowly pondering them, praying them, and seeking to join Paul in living them.

Whether Paul was in prison for two years and released, or kept in prison until his death, the earliest church traditions place Paul's death around A.D. 64 or 65 and, as noted above, associate it with Nero's persecution of Christians after the Great Fire of Rome.

In mid-July A.D. 64, a fire broke out in the city of Rome, destroying much of the city and leaving hundreds of thousands homeless.* Some speculated that Emperor Nero himself had hired thugs to start the fire so he could redesign and rebuild the city to his liking. Others discounted that idea. Regardless of how the fire started, it consumed much of the city. The Roman historian Tacitus writes,

> And so, to get rid of this rumor [that he had hired henchmen to set fire to the city], Nero set up as the culprits and punished with the utmost refinement of cruelty a class hated for their abominations, who are commonly called Christians. Christus, from whom their name is derived, was executed at the hands of the procurator Pontius Pilate in the reign of Tiberius. Checked for a moment, this pernicious superstition again broke out, not only in Judea, the source of the evil, but even in Rome....Accordingly, arrest was first made of those who confessed; then, on their evidence, an immense multitude was convicted, not so much on the charge of arson as because of [their] hatred for the human race. Besides being put to death they were made to serve as objects of amusement; they were clothed in the hides of beasts and torn to death by dogs; others were crucified, others set on fire to serve to illuminate the night when daylight failed. Nero had thrown open his grounds for the display, and was putting on a show in the circus, where he mingled with the people in the dress of charioteer or drove about in his chariot. All this gave rise to a feeling of pity, even towards men whose guilt merited the most exemplary punishment; for it was felt that they were being destroyed not for the public good but to gratify the cruelty of an individual.†

Among the first people arrested were the leaders of the Christian faith. According to tradition, both Peter and Paul were in Rome during this period, though possibly some months apart. Then, upon being convicted, each spent time in the

* Sources date this either July 16, 18, or 19 and some say it happened in the morning, others at night.

† Tacitus, *Annals* (XV.44). Tacitus was a boy when this occurred.

The Mamertine Prison, where tradition says that Peter and Paul spent time before their executions

Mamertine Prison, located on Capitoline Hill and used for hundreds of years before and after the time of Paul. It is among the most dramatic places to visit in Rome when remembering Paul's story.

Entering the main room at the Mamertine Prison, visitors can see ancient frescoes on the walls showing Peter and Paul. This main room, located below grade, has what appears at first glance to be a manhole that opens into a lower level. In ancient times it was not uncommon for a dungeon or prison to be accessed through such an opening, with prisoners lowered by harness or rope into the dungeon below.

Steps have been created to the lower dungeon. Descending the steps, one comes to a dark and damp room. I've been there several times, and though I did not measure the room, my recollection is that it is about thirty feet long and twenty feet wide, with a ceiling height of perhaps twelve feet. In the past visitors stood on the floor, but now a walkway has been constructed above the floor. In the ceiling is the "manhole" through which prisoners were lowered. On one wall is an altar commemorating

Peter's crucifixion. A hole in the rock floor still contains water that springs from the ground. Several traditions exist about this water, among them that Peter and Paul, in the prison at different times, used the water to baptize their fellow prisoners.

Was Paul consigned to this prison before his death? We can't know for sure. But being in this place connects us to his final days. On my first visit I waited until no one else was in the room and asked if the lights could be turned off. I sat in the darkness, as I imagined Paul might have sat, with only the light streaming in from the hole in the ceiling. I pictured him writing what may have been his final letter, dictating to Luke or another friend who sat above the manhole and who wrote as Paul spoke the words we find in 2 Timothy 4:6-8 (CEB):

> I'm already being poured out like a sacrifice to God, and the time of my death is near. I have fought the good fight, finished the race, and kept the faith. At last the champion's wreath that is awarded for righteousness is waiting for me.

This is a prison cell located under the Church of Santa Maria Scala Coeli in Rome, adjacent to the location where Paul is believed to have been executed. The tradition is that Paul was moved from the Mamertine Prison to this prison cell just prior to his beheading.

Paul may have felt abandoned by some he had mentored, but the words in 2 Timothy bear witness to a man who, to the end, trusted in the gospel he had preached and in God's ultimate victory over evil. The letter ends with these words: "The Lord will rescue me from every evil action and will save me for his heavenly kingdom. To him be the glory forever and always. Amen" (2 Timothy 4:18 CEB).

Paul's Death

At this point, since Scripture does not record Paul's final hours and death, we turn to the traditions of the church. The tradition is that Paul was taken from the Mamertine Prison to the place of his execution, what is known today as San Paolo alle Tre Fontane—the Church of St. Paul at the Three Fountains. This church is one of three important churches located at the Tre Fontane Abbey, also known as the Abbey of Saints Vincent and Anastasius. One of the churches on this site is called Santa Maria Scala Coeli (St. Mary of the Stairway to Heaven). Beneath this church is a prison cell that, tradition tells us, was the last place where Paul was held before his execution.

The earliest written testimony we have about Paul's death comes from a nonbiblical source, a document known as 1 Clement (though it does not mention Clement by name) and which likely was written sometime in the A.D. 90s. In this letter written to the church at Corinth, the author refers to Paul (1 Clement 5:5-7) but does not tell us how Paul died. It is the apocryphal Acts of Paul, written about 160, that tells us Paul was beheaded for his faith after testifying to the gospel before Nero. There we read, "Then Paul stood with his face to the east and lifted up his hands unto heaven and prayed a long time, and in his prayer he conversed in the Hebrew tongue with the fathers,

St. Paul at the Three Fountains (Tre Fontane) is the church built atop the traditional site of Paul's execution. On the left interior wall are three niches through which worshipers may look to see the three fountains that are said to have sprung up where Paul's head "bounced" after his execution.

and then stretched forth his neck without speaking."* The executioner then beheaded Paul.

A later, very graphic tradition says that Paul's head bounced three times upon striking the ground, and in each place that his head bounced, a spring or fountain came up from the ground. Though the three fountains actually predate the time of Paul, this early tradition anchors Paul's death at the location of the Church of St. Paul at the Three Fountains. If you go to the church today, on the long wall across from the main entrance you'll see the three fountains, underground springs whose water still runs. There are grates that prevent worshipers from touching or drinking the water, but the water can be seen and heard by worshipers. Various works of art throughout the church testify to Paul's death (and Peter's as well).

If you travel to Rome to retrace Paul's story, you'll also want to visit the Basilica of St. Paul Outside the Walls, mentioned

* *The Acts of Paul,* at least what remains of this ancient document, can be read at http://www.earlychristianwritings.com/text/actspaul.html. A description of Paul's death can be found in section X paragraph V.

Basilica of St. Paul Outside the Walls, built atop the site of Paul's burial

previously as the traditional location of Paul's burial. One of four major churches in Rome, it is massive, easily able to hold several thousand worshipers (as contrasted with Tre Fontane, which holds only several hundred). The basilica was originally built by the Emperor Constantine in the 300s, over the place that Christians had venerated as Paul's grave for as far back as anyone could remember.

After Paul's death, he would have been buried by his many friends in Rome. When he died there were hundreds, perhaps thousands of Christians in Rome. Paul may have been buried in a stone or clay coffin or sarcophagus. It is likely that Christians would have marked and visited the site of Paul's grave. In 390 Emperor Theodosius placed Paul's remains in a new sarcophagus. The sarcophagus was believed to have been reburied in 433 when part of the church was destroyed and rebuilt following an earthquake. A marble slab was placed atop the sarcophagus at that time and engraved with the words *Paulo Apostolo Mart*—Paul the Apostle, Martyr. The church was destroyed and rebuilt several more times over the centuries, with the main altar built above the marble slab. In 1823 a fire destroyed much of the church. When it was rebuilt, the marble slab that had previously been visible under the altar was covered and a new altar built atop this.*

In 2002 Vatican archaeologists were given permission to excavate around and under the main altar of the church. They found the marble slab that had been covered after the fire of 1823. Next they found the 1,600-year-old sarcophagus where Theodosius had placed Paul's remains. One side of the sarcophagus is now visible to visitors as they approach the altar. The archaeologists opened a hole into the sarcophagus and inside found small bone fragments and "traces of a precious linen cloth, purple in color, laminated with pure gold, and a blue colored textile with filaments of linen." The bones were subjected to carbon dating, which revealed they were from the first or second century.[1]

Paul's Legacy

Of course Paul's burial was not the end of his story. The churches he founded, the converts he made, the letters he wrote, and the theological reflections he left behind would become the driving force of the Christian faith. People would seek to do as he had commanded the Corinthians: "Follow my example, just like I follow Christ's" (1 Corinthians 11:1 CEB). Much of Christian theology would be shaped by his words. No one, aside from Jesus himself, would have a greater impact upon the Christian faith.

There is another sense in which Paul's burial was not the end of his story. Paul proclaimed that, "to me, living is Christ and dying is gain" (Philippians 1:21). Paul described his perspective on suffering, persecution, and death:

* To read the story of the excavations see Maria Cristina Valsecchi, "Saint Paul's Tomb Unearthed," *National Geographic News*, December 11, 2006, http://news.nationalgeographic.com/news/2006/12/061211-saint-paul.html.

> So we do not lose heart. Even though our outer nature is wasting away, our inner nature is being renewed day by day. For this slight momentary affliction is preparing us for an eternal weight of glory beyond all measure…We know that if the earthly tent we live in is destroyed, we have a building from God, a house not made with hands, eternal in the heavens. (2 Corinthians 4:16-17; 5:1)

Paul's perspective on life was captured in these well-loved words that close the eighth chapter of Romans:

> If God is for us, who is against us?…Who will separate us from the love of Christ? Will hardship, or distress, or persecution, or famine, or nakedness, or peril, or sword?…No, in all these things we are more than conquerors through him who loved us. For I am convinced that neither death, nor life, nor angels, nor rulers, nor things present, nor things to come, nor powers, nor height, nor depth, nor anything else in all creation, will be able to separate us from the love of God in Christ Jesus our Lord. (Romans 8:31, 35, 37-39)

Perhaps Paul's perspective on death in the light of Christ's resurrection is best captured by his citation of Isaiah 25:8 when writing to the Corinthians, "Death has been swallowed up in victory" (1 Corinthians 15:54).

As I started writing this book I went to the ICU to visit Susan, a woman at the church I serve. I had baptized Susan and her children twenty years earlier, and since that time they had played an active part in the church. She had just learned that the doctors had done everything they could do to treat her and that her time was short. I met her husband and children at the hospital to anoint her with oil and to pray with Susan and her family as we entrusted her to God's care.

When I opened my Bible, I turned to Paul's words: "Death has been swallowed up in victory." "To live is Christ and to die is gain." "When this life is over we have a building not made with hands, eternal in the heavens."

I reminded Susan of the words I speak every year at the close of the Easter sermon. When people sometimes ask me, "Do you really believe this stuff? Do you believe that Jesus rose from the dead and that death is not the end for us?" My congregation knows these words by heart and usually joins me in whispering them as I say them each year. As we sat in the hospital Susan joined me in repeating: "I not only believe it; I'm counting on it."

Paul was counting on it.

Responding to the Call

I titled this book *The Call* because that word captures Paul's life so well. On the Damascus Road, Christ called him to lay aside his own hopes and dreams and to follow. Christ called him to take the gospel to the Gentile world. Christ called him to live a life wholly surrendered to God. Christ called him to preach and to suffer. Christ called him to experience danger and risk, great joy and peace. My aim in writing the book was in part to study the life and faith of the Apostle Paul. But it was also to invite you to be inspired by his life, that you too might hear God's call and respond as Paul did. I'd like to end with a picture of what that looks like today.

While in Johannesburg, South Africa, I went to visit one of our church's mission partners, a preschool located ninety minutes outside the city in an "informal settlement"—a village at the edge of the city trash dump consisting of shacks built from corrugated tin, cardboard, plastic, and plywood found among the trash. Sixteen thousand people live there, in what some call a "shantytown" and others a "squatters village." There's no electricity, no sewers, no water. We walked among the shacks until we came to one of the few substantial buildings in the settlement, the preschool we help to fund. There are thirty teachers and other employees, hired from the settlement and living among the 240 children they serve. The children are guaranteed at least one nutritious meal each day. They are provided health care and immunizations, and they learn the same things that children in American preschools learn, in hopes that after preschool these kids might have a chance to actually go to school. Education is their ticket out.

The situation might seem overwhelming to many, but not to Isabelle. She is a trained social worker and a committed follower of Jesus Christ. I'm guessing she's in her midforties, and she has devoted the last seven years of her life to developing the preschool. I asked Isabelle what compelled her to show up in this place, where the smell from the dump wafts into her preschool. Tears welled up in her eyes. She told me that at the age of fourteen she heard a call from God, a call to do something with her life that would change the world. She was trained as a social worker and knew she wanted to serve the poor. She came to this place and knew God needed her there. It is that call that keeps her going, helping people and watching their lives be changed.

Your call may not be as dramatic as the Apostle Paul's. It may be not be as noble as Isabelle's. But you have been called and continue to be called by Christ. You're called to follow him daily in your life. You're called to be an instrument of his love and grace. You're called to live, give, and serve. As you answer that call, you will find that your own life and the world are changed forever.

If you still have doubts about your call, consider the words of my friend Paul Rasmussen, who pastors Highland Park United Methodist Church in Dallas. He routinely asks his congregation, "What won't happen if you don't do what God has called you to do?"

What wouldn't have happened if Isabelle hadn't answered God's call? What wouldn't have happened if Paul hadn't answered that call?

What won't happen if you don't do what God has called you to do?

NOTES

Chapter 1

1. David Capes, Rodney Reeves, E. Randolph Richards, eds., *Rediscovering Paul* (Downers Grove, IL: InterVarsity Press, 2007), 42–43.
2. Strabo, *Geography*, Book XIV, 3:13.
3. See Stanley Porter's essay on "Paul and the Greco-Roman Educational System" in *As It Is Written: Studying Paul's Use of Scripture*, eds. Stanley E. Porter and Christopher D. Porter (Atlanta: Society of Biblical Literature, 2008), 99–105.
4. Mishnah, Sanhedrin 6:1-4. This description is found in the *Zondervan Illustrated Bible Encyclopedia*, ed. Clinton Arnold (Grand Rapids: Zondervan, 2003).
5. Dave Wilkinson, http://mppres.org/sermons/2007/Jan21.htm, Jan. 21, 2007.
6. For a more detailed discussion on this kind of labeling, see chapter 2 of *The Literary Construction of the Other in the Acts of the Apostles* by Mitzi Smith (Eugene, OR: Wipf and Stock Publishers, 2011).

Chapter 3

1. See Keener's discussion of the Noahide laws in *Acts: An Exegetical Commentary,* vol. 3, Kindle ed. (Grand Rapids: Baker, 2014), starting at Kindle location 5347.
2. *The Apostolic Tradition* 21:16
3. The text of the complete manuscript of the Didache (also called The Teaching of the Twelve) can be found online at http://www.earlychristianwritings.com/text/didache-roberts.html. The translation I've cited is from this online version.

Chapter 4

1. Georges Raepsaet and Mike Tolley (1993), "Le Diolkos de l'Isthme à Corinthe: son tracé, son fonctionnement", *Bulletin de Correspondance Hellénique* 117: pp. 252ff, 257–61; doi:10.3406/bch.1993.1679.
5. Zlatko Mandzuka, *Demistifying the Odyssey* (Bloomington, Ind: AuthorHouse UK Ltd, 2013), 241.
6. Strabo, *Geography,* viii, 6, 20, 22.

Chapter 6

1. Stephen Brown, "Pope says bone fragments found in St. Paul's tomb," Reuters, June 28, 2009. http://www.reuters.com/article/2009/06/28/us-italy-saint-bone-idUSTRE55R22O20090628.

Image Credits

Unless otherwise noted, images courtesy of Adam Hamilton.

Images pages 19 and 100 courtesy of A.D. Riddle/Bibleplaces.com.

Image page 20 courtesy of Teogomez/Wikimedia.org.

Images pages 28, 77, 79, 92, 99, 100, 144 and 214 courtesy of Todd Bolen/Bibleplaces.com.

Image page 29 courtesy of JanSmith/Flicker.com. See https://creativecommons.org/licenses/by/2.0/ for restrictions.

Image page 39 courtesy of bumihills/Shutterstock.com.

Images pages 42 courtesy of gezgin01/iStock.com and tunart/iStock.com.

Images pages 172 courtesy of ZU_09/iStock.com.

Image page 184 courtesy of Flik47/Shutterstock.com.

Image page 200 courtesy of pavel068/Shutterstock.com.

BIBLIOGRAPHY

Arnold, Clinton E., ed. *Zondervan Illustrated Bible Backgrounds Commentary. Vol. 2, John, Acts.* Grand Rapids: Zondervan, 2002.

Bird, Michael F., ed. *Four Views on the Apostle Paul*. Grand Rapids: Zondervan, 2012.

Bruce, F. F. *Paul: Apostle of the Heart Set Free*. Grand Rapids: Eerdmans, 1977.

—— *The New International Commentary of the New Testament: The Book of the Acts.* Rev. ed. Grand Rapids: Eerdmans, 1988.

Capes, David, Rodney Reeves, E. Randolph Richards, eds. *Rediscovering Paul*. Downers Grove, IL: InterVarsity Press, 2007.

Cimok, Faith. *Journeys of Paul: From Tarsus to the Ends of the Earth*. Istanbul, Turkey: Mumhane Caddesi Mangir Sokak, 2012.

Dibelius, Martin, and Werner Georg Kummel, eds. *Paul*. Philadelphia: Westminster Press, 1953.

Drane, John. *Paul: An Illustrated Documentary.* New York: Harper & Row, 1976

Dunn, James D. G. *The Theology of Paul the Apostle*. Grand Rapids: Eerdmans, 1998.

Fant, Clyde E., and Mitchell G. Reddish. *A Guide to Biblical Sites in Greece and Turkey*. New York: Oxford University Press, 2003.

Gunther, Bornkamm. *Paul*. New York: Harper & Row, 1969.

Keck, Leander E., ed. *The New Interpreter's Bible: A Commentary in Twelve Volumes. Vol. 10. Acts, Introduction To Epistolary Literature, Romans, 1 Corinthians*. Nashville: Abingdon Press, 2002.

Keener, Craig S. *Acts: An Exegetical Commentary*. Vol. 3. Grand Rapids: Baker Academic, 2014.

Longenecker, Bruce W., and Todd D. Still. *Thinking Through Paul: A Survey of His Life, Letters, and Theology*. Grand Rapids: Zondervan, 2014.

Mandzuka, Zlatko. *Demistifying the Odyssey* (Bloomington, Ind: AuthorHouse UK Ltd, 2013.

Peterson, David G. *The Acts of the Apostles: The Pillar New Testament Commentary*. Grand Rapids: Eerdmans, 2009.

Porter, Stanley E. "Paul and the Greco-Roman Educational System. " In *As It Is Written: Studying Paul's Use of Scripture*. Edited by Stanley E. Porter and Christopher D. Porter. Atlanta: Society of Biblical Literature, 2008.

Ramsey, William M. *St. Paul: The Traveler and Roman Citizen.* Grand Rapids: Kregel Publications, 2001.

Reicke, Bo. "Caesarea, Rome, and the Captivity Epistles. " In *Apostolic History and the Gospel: Biblical and Historical Essays Presented to F .F. Bruce*. Edited by W. Ward Gasque and Ralph P. Martin. Exeter: Paternoster Press, 1970.

Smith, Mitzi. *The Literary Construction of the Other in the Acts of the Apostles: Charismatics, the Jews, and Women.* Eugene, OR: Wipf & Stock, 2011.

Willimon, William H. *Acts: Interpretation, A Bible Commentary for Teaching and Preaching*. Louisville: Westminster John Knox Press, 1988.

Wilson, Mark. *Biblical Turkey: A Guide to the Jewish and Christian Sites of Asia Minor.* Istanbul, Turkey: Yayinlari, 2012.

Wright, N. T. *Paul and the Faithfulness of God*, Book 1, Parts 1 & 2; Book 2, Parts 3 & 4. Minneapolis: Fortress Press, 2013.

ACKNOWLEDGMENTS

This book and the accompanying video, leader guide, and children and youth studies have been a collaborative project, with so many exceptional people helping to make it happen.

I'm grateful to James Ridgeway and his team at Educational Opportunities Tours, who provided our travel arrangements, accommodations, and guides for the journey to Turkey, Greece, and Italy. They were a key part of making this project a reality.

Special thanks to our guides. Hakan Bashar traveled across Turkey with us and provided a wealth of information. Kostas Tsevas traveled with us across Greece and was a walking history book, shedding light on the Greece and Macedonia of Paul's time. And Antonio Scona and Ruggero Scoma were a gift in Rome, as they helped us navigate our way through the city and gain access to the important places on Paul's journey.

I'd also like to thank the Lilly Endowment for awarding me a Clergy Renewal Grant, which provided a portion of the funds for the journey in Paul's footsteps.

Lee Rudeen and Natalie Cleveland traveled with me to the lands of Paul and captured the entire journey on video. They are both outstanding videographers and really terrific people.

I consider it a privilege to work with them. Natalie then tirelessly edited the videos accompanying this book. I'm proud of the amazing work she did in piecing the videos together from the hours of footage we shot. My wife, LaVon Hamilton, and Lee's wife, Anne Rudeen, each assisted with the filming of the project in a host of ways. I am indebted to them. My assistant, Sue Thompson, helped in coordinating my schedule and in preparing the bibliography based on the resources I drew upon for this study.

I'm grateful for Dr. Mark Wilson, director of the Asia Minor Research Center, who read the manuscript and offered important suggestions and corrections.

The Ministry Resources team at Abingdon Press were invaluable partners in the production of the program. Without their work, *The Call* would not have seen the light of day. Thank you to Susan Salley, Ron Kidd, Sally Sharpe, Tim Cobb, Marcia Myatt, Alan Vermilye, Tracey Craddock, Camilla Myers, and Sonia Worsham.

Finally, I'd like to thank my congregation, The United Methodist Church of the Resurrection, for allowing me the time to work on projects such as this one. I am proud to be their pastor, and I'm grateful for their vision of encouraging other congregations.

Educational Opportunities Tours

I would like to thank Educational Opportunities Tours (EO) for their support of the work and travel that made this book possible.

Educational Opportunities has worked closely with me for more than fifteen years, beginning with my first journey to the Holy Land, continuing with my trip through the British Isles to follow in the footsteps of John Wesley, and on my recent trip to Italy, Turkey, and Greece to trace the ministry of the Apostle Paul. Their advice and support have helped us invite you, the reader, along for these journeys, walking the road to Bethlehem, seeing the sites of Jesus' last hours, following the life of Wesley, and traveling to many of the destinations of the Apostle Paul. EO provides valuable advice and counsel when my team and I travel, and I eagerly anticipate the planning of our next trip.

–Adam Hamilton

For more information, go to www.eo.TravelWithUs.com.

The Journey

Journey with Adam Hamilton as he travels from Nazareth to Bethlehem in this fascinating look at the birth of Jesus Christ. As he did with Jesus' crucifixion in *24 Hours That Changed the World*, Hamilton once again approaches a world-changing event with thoughtfulness. Using historical information, archaeological data, and a personal look at some of the stories surrounding the birth, the most amazing moment in history will become more real and heartfelt as you walk along this road.

Read *The Journey* on your own or,
for a more in-depth study,
enjoy it with a small group.

ISBN 978-1-4267-1425-2

AVAILABLE WHEREVER FINE BOOKS ARE SOLD.

FOR MORE INFORMATION ABOUT ADAM HAMILTON, VISIT WWW.ADAMHAMILTON.ORG

Continue the Journey

Go deeper on your Christmas journey with *A Season of Reflection*. With Scripture, stories, and prayer, this collection of 28 daily readings brings the well-known story into your daily spiritual life.

ISBN 978-1-4267-1426-9

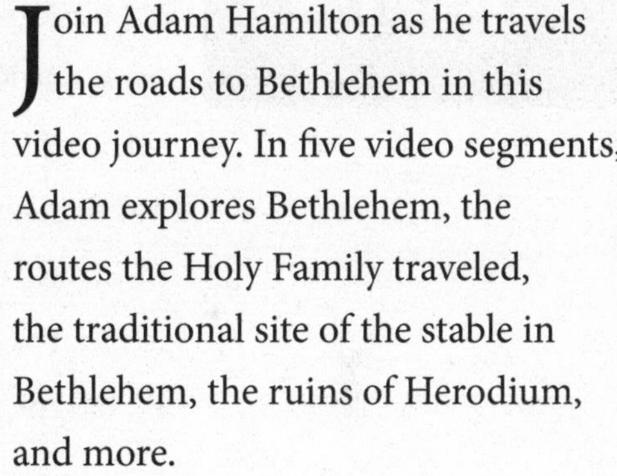

Join Adam Hamilton as he travels the roads to Bethlehem in this video journey. In five video segments, Adam explores Bethlehem, the routes the Holy Family traveled, the traditional site of the stable in Bethlehem, the ruins of Herodium, and more.

ISBN 978-1-4267-1999-8

Study resources for children and youth and an app for families are also available.

Learn more at JourneyThisChristmas.com

AVAILABLE WHEREVER FINE BOOKS ARE SOLD.

FOR MORE INFORMATION ABOUT ADAM HAMILTON, VISIT WWW.ADAMHAMILTON.ORG

The Way

Travel to the Holy Land in this third volume of Adam Hamilton's Bible study trilogy on the life of Jesus. Once again, Hamilton approaches his subject matter with thoughtfulness and wisdom as he did with Jesus' crucifixion in *24 Hours That Changed the World* and with Jesus' birth in *The Journey*. Using historical background, archaeological findings, and stories of the faith, Hamilton retraces the footsteps of Jesus from his baptism to the temptations to the heart of his ministry, including the people he loved, the enemies he made, the parables he taught, and the roads that he traveled.

Read *The Way* on your own or,
for a more in-depth study,
enjoy it with a small group.

ISBN 978-1-4267-5251-3

AVAILABLE WHEREVER FINE BOOKS ARE SOLD.

FOR MORE INFORMATION ABOUT ADAM HAMILTON, VISIT WWW.ADAMHAMILTON.ORG

Continue the Way

This companion volume to *The Way* functions beautifully on its own or as part of the churchwide experience. Adam Hamilton offers daily devotions that enable us to pause, meditate, and emerge changed forever. Ideal for use during Lent, the reflections include Scripture, stories from Hamilton's own ministry, and prayers.

ISBN 978-1-4267-5252-0

Join Adam Hamilton in the Holy Land as he retraces the life and ministry of Jesus Christ in this DVD study. Perfect for adult and youth classes, the DVD includes a Leader Guide to facilitate small group discussion about the book, the devotions, and the DVD. Each session averages ten minutes.

ISBN 978-1-4267-5253-7

Study resources for children and youth are also available.

Available wherever fine books are sold.

For more information about Adam Hamilton, visit www.AdamHamilton.org

24 Hours That Changed the World

Walk with Jesus on his final day.
Sit beside him at the Last Supper.
Pray with him in Gethsemane.
Follow him to the cross.
Desert him. Deny him.
Experience the Resurrection.

No single event in human history has received more attention than the suffering and crucifixion of Jesus of Nazareth. In this heartbreaking, inspiring book, Adam Hamilton guides us, step by step, through the last 24 hours of Jesus' life.

ISBN 978-0-687-46555-2

"Adam Hamilton combines biblical story, historical detail, theological analysis, spiritual insight, and pastoral warmth to retell the narrative of Jesus' last and greatest hours."
—**Leith Anderson,** author of *The Jesus Revolution*

Available wherever fine books are sold.
For more information about Adam Hamilton, visit www.AdamHamilton.org

Devotions and Study Resources

For the Lent and Easter season, Adam Hamilton offers 40 days of devotions enabling us to pause, reflect, dig deeper, and emerge from the experience changed forever.

ISBN 978-1-4267-0031-6

Travel with Adam through this companion DVD visiting the sites, walking where Jesus walked along the road that led to the pain and triumph of the cross.

The DVD includes seven sessions plus an introduction and bonus clips. Each session averages ten minutes.

ISBN 978-0-687-65970-8

Also available:
Older and Younger Children's study sessions
and youth small group resources

AVAILABLE WHEREVER FINE BOOKS ARE SOLD.

FOR MORE INFORMATION ABOUT ADAM HAMILTON, VISIT WWW.ADAMHAMILTON.ORG